OLD WORLDS FOR NEW

Old Worlds for New

A Study of the Post-Industrial State

By

Arthur J. Penty

Author of "The Restoration of the Guild System"

NEW YORK: SUNWISE TURN, Inc. 2 EAST 31st St
LONDON : GEORGE ALLEN & UNWIN LTD.
RUSKIN HOUSE 40 MUSEUM STREET, W.C. 1

First published in 1917

TO

E. T.

PREFACE

THE scope of this volume is suggested by its title : *Old Worlds for New; a Study of the Post-Industrial State*, for it suggests at once the paradox which lies at the centre of our social life—that in order to go forward it is necessary to look back. This truth, which was apparent to many in the period before the war, is more apparent to-day. It needs little insight into social and political questions to realize that the war marks the close of an era in our civilization, and that the task of social reconstruction can no longer be delayed. After the war, when the artificial and unnatural prosperity which we now enjoy is over, all the glaring contradictions of our civilization will stand out before us, naked in their ugliness, and woe betide us if in that supreme crisis the mind of the nation is still unprepared. For no despot alone, however great, can save society. The success of any measures which he might initiate for the public good is conditioned and limited in every direction by the general level of thought and intelligence of the community.

Recognizing, then, the extreme gravity of the

situation and the importance of meeting the impending crisis with well ascertained and clearly defined principles, I am seeking now, by the publication in book form of a series of articles written for the *Daily Herald* in the months immediately preceding the outbreak of war, to secure a wider recognition for certain fundamental principles of social organization which in our day have fallen into desuetude. Their revival, I am convinced, must precede the task of social reconstruction. The experience of the war has not shaken, but has confirmed, my belief in their truth ; indeed, the war itself I cannot but regard as evidence in support of them. It is the inevitable catastrophic ending of a society which has chosen to deny the law of its own being.

Though the text of the articles has been revised for publication in a more permanent form, it remains substantially unaltered. Owing to the outbreak of the war the series came to a premature end ; and in consequence the last four now appear for the first time. As the reader will gather from the first article, they were written as an attempt to formulate a new policy for that section of the Socialist movement which was losing its faith in the all-sufficiency of the gospel of Collectivism. As such they failed in their more immediate purpose. By general consent a system of Local Guilds which I advocated was deemed not immediately practicable. With that decision I am in full accord. Nowadays I can see only too clearly that the gulf which separates such a system from practical politics is, at the moment, too wide to be bridged, and that the National Guild policy, with its demand for the abolition of the Wage System, is the one for to-day. But National Guilds can have no finality about them. Once the workers find themselves in the possession of industry the fundamental contradictions which underlie industrialism will demand a solution, and that demand will set us on the road to Local Guilds. " The old ideas," once said Mr. Chesterton, " are coming in again ; but they are coming in walking backwards." That is the way in which the Guild idea advances to-day. Under the guise of National Guilds, a step backward is being taken by men who for the most part fail to realize that industrialism is doomed to dissolution and decay.

For my changed attitude on this issue the war is responsible. Hitherto I had supposed that society was to be reconstructed by peaceable means —at any rate under the normal conditions which peace presupposes—for though I recognized the possibility of revolution, it did not appear to me to be in any way imminent. Under such conditions the National Guild proposal, to carry the citadel of capitalism by assault, appeared to me to be rather impracticable. Capitalism, I thought, would have to be undermined ; it would never yield to a frontal attack. But the war has altered the factors of the problem. Capitalism no longer appears impregnable. Indeed, I feel the war by its reactions will break it up, and in all proba-

bility precipitate a revolution. In this light the
National Guild propaganda acquires a new significance. The fact of the war has brought it
within the range of practical politics, for what
was impossible in times of peace may be possible
in a time of revolution.

Meanwhile political development tends to con-
firm my belief in the truth of the old principles of
social organization. Considering that these principles are antipathetic to those of Collectivism,
and that the State is to be seen everywhere increasing its hold—that railways, shipping, endless
factories and coalfields have come under Government control, and that it is more than probable
that circumstances after the war will increasingly
compel the State to interfere in the management
of industry, it may not unreasonably be asked
what grounds I have for 'such confidence. To this
I answer that, apart from the coalfields, which may
eventually be nationalized, and to State ownership
of natural monopolies, to which there can be no
objection, it will be seen as the present scheme
of things unfolds that this State activity does not
tend towards the collectivization of industry, but
towards a revival of the Guilds. That confusion
should exist on this point is due to the fact that
all State action in relation to industry has quite
unreasonably come to be regarded as Collectivist.
Such, however, is far from being the case.
Whether Governmental interference with industry
is to be regarded as Collectivist or not, all depends
upon the nature of the interference itself. If its

aim be to take the direction of industry out of
private hands and to place it in the hands of
officials, then it is Collectivist ; but if, on the
contrary, its aim be to protect the public or the
workers against capitalist abuses, then the State
is merely resuming the functions which in the
Middle Ages were performed by the Guilds, and
which in the future will be performed by the
revived Guilds. Once embarked upon a policy
of regulating prices the State will, as the system
extends, find itself compelled to seek the re-
creation of the Guilds in order to give practical
effect to its intentions.

Fixed prices, then, is a path to the Guilds.
This is a certainty, for in this connection history
is repeating itself. It was to guard society against
the evils of an unregulated currency that the
Guilds were instituted in the past. The Guild
legislators realized that a currency, when unregulated, lent itself to manipulation for profit, and
being determined to restrict currency to its legitimate use as a medium of exchange, they sought
a remedy in fixed prices. Once grasp the
economic necessity of fixed prices and the whole
range of Guild regulations becomes intelligible.
In order to fix prices, it becomes necessary to
maintain a standard of quality. As a standard of
quality cannot be defined finally in the terms of
law, it is necessary, in order to uphold a standard,
to place authority in the hands of craft masters—
a consensus of opinion among whom constitutes the
final Court of Appeal. In order to ensure a

supply of masters it is necessary to train apprentices, to regulate the size of the workshop, hours of labour, the volume of production, and the like. The first link in this chain of economic necessity has already been forged, the rest is only a matter of time.

The force which is driving things in this direction is, at the moment, " rising prices." After the war other forces will make themselves felt. The tendency to-day towards servile conditions of labour has its counterpart in the growth of " industrial unrest," and it needs but the unemployed problem which will follow the war, if not immediately, then in a year or two, to open wide the floodgates of anarchy and revolution. Confronted with this, our statesmen will be helpless, for they lack any comprehension of the problem of our society as a whole. Politicians have for so long been concerned with secondary things in society, while discussions of primary and fundamental principles were at such a discount, that they are without the mental equipment which a great crisis demands. Evidence of their lack of grip on reality is forthcoming on every hand. Though they realize that the demobilization of the forces and the closing down of the munition factories will bring upon us an unemployed problem on an unprecedented scale, and though they are proposing certain measures for coping with it, they yet remain for the most part unconscious of the real peril that confronts them, consoling themselves with the comforting thought that, bad as things are likely to be, the dislocation of industry will only be temporary, and that the unemployed problem will tend to disappear before the anticipated revival of trade.

That there are real grounds for any such optimism is to be doubted. That trade will not revive after the war may perhaps be difficult to prove, but there are many reasons for believing that such will be the case. It would appear that the limits of industrial expansion (a further increase of which is essential to a revival of trade, if industry is to remain on its present basis) was reached before the war ; and that the war itself was the direct consequence of the economic *impasse* which had been created. Professor Hauser [1] tells us in this connection that in Germany the ratio of productivity, due to never-slackening energy, technique, and scientific development, was before the war far outstripping the ratio of demand. Production was no longer controlled by demand, but by plant. What the Americans call overhead expenses had increased to such an enormous extent that no furnace could be damped down and no machine stopped ; for the overhead expenses would then eat up the profits, and the whole industrial organization come crashing down, bringing with it national bankruptcy. To avert this impending catastrophe, the Germans chose to resort to war. We miss the lesson which this war should teach us, if we think

[1] *Germany's Commercial Grip of the World*, by Professor Hauser (Eveleigh Nash).

that their watchword, " World power or down-fall," was merely the product of a 'diseased imagination. The truth is, it had become for them an economic necessity. It was a desperate effort to escape from the consequences of un-regulated machine production.

I insist upon a frank recognition of this fact, for our natural and justifiable disgust at the arrogance of Prussian militarism appears to have entirely blinded us to the ugly economic facts which lay behind the war. The anti-climax in which unregulated production in Germany had ended would, apart from the war, not only before long have overtaken us, but the whole of Western civilization. For industrialism was everywhere travelling along the same road, and I do not exaggerate when I say that so far as our welfare and happiness are concerned, it is a matter of life and death with us that this fact should be publicly recognized. If discussion to-day is to be taken as any indication of the policy which we are to pursue after the war, we appear to be heading blindfold to disaster. Nowhere do I see any recognition of the ugly fact that the industrial system has reached its limit of expansion. On the contrary, our policy for after the war, a cynic might say, is to make bad worse—to reproduce, in fact, in an intensified form, the very conditions which have brought the war about.

The economic isolation of Germany, on which our faith for the future is based, is to be recom-mended just to the extent that it is in the interests of every country to be as self-contained as possible. But such a policy fails to touch the central issue of over-production, which will be staring us in the face after the war.[1] It is admitted that we shall have to face a decreased purchasing power among all the belligerent nations. This of itself is sufficient to precipitate catastrophe, when we remember that our industries can only be made to pay on the assumption that we can dispose of our goods in ever increasing quantities. But where shall we be if the advance guards of industrialism get their own way with their policy of still further extending the volume of production by increased specialization? Clearly it can only make matters worse. Such a policy, instead of helping us to solve our unemployed problem, can only intensify it. For the organization of industry on a basis of " scientific management " will not increase, but decrease the demand for labour.[2] The old Manchester School doctrine that a reduction of prices (at which this policy aims) will be followed by an increase of demand will not hold good after the war, because it presupposes, among other things, that the major part of the nation is already in employment.

[1] This problem will be aggravated by the shortage of shipping which is resulting from the submarine campaign and will popularly be entirely ascribed to it.

[2] In the Minority Report of the Poor Law Commission Mr. and Mrs. Webb say: "There is no denying that nowadays machinery is displacing labour." If this was true before the war, how much more so will it be after it, quite apart from " scientific management."

Such, then, is the dilemma which will confront us, and I should imagine that the only conclusion to which any rational person could come would be that, if going forward can only lead us to further disasters, we must make up our minds to go back. How long it will take us to swallow our pride and come to that decision I do not know ; but come to it finally we must, for there is no alternative. What I fear, however, is that instead of courageously facing the issue in a bold and constructive way, such as a frank recognition of the fact that the days of unregulated production are over might beget, we shall stupidly pursue a dual policy of seeking on the one hand by labour-saving machinery and " scientific management " to reduce the wage bill, and on the other to deal with the consequent unemployment by means of State subsidies and private philanthropy. The result will be that we shall get nowhere in particular, or, what is more than probable, that we shall embark on new military enterprises in a vain endeavour to restore to society some of the apparent prosperity which accompanies the war to-day.

I said that if further disasters are to be averted, we shall have to make up our minds to go back. But, comes the question, how? The answer is simplicity itself—by the reversal of our economic policy. To the popular mind such a reversal connotes nothing more than the abandonment of the principles of Free Trade in favour of Protection. But the issue of Free Trade and Protection is not the central issue. Like all the issues in current politics, it is on the circumference of things. Free Trade or Protection will not of itself effect a fundamental change. The rich will still continue to invest their surplus wealth for further increase on the assumption not only that their private fortunes will be thereby enlarged, but that such investment gives employment. One hundred and fifty years ago, when this doctrine was first enunciated, there was perhaps something in it. But it certainly is not true to-day, when the investment of surplus wealth for further increase in most cases has the very opposite effect. It decreases employment, and it decreases it because the aim of most new business enterprises to-day is to supplant the man by the machine. It does not to-day increase the national wealth, but the overhead expenses of industry, which, by making our industrial system more and more top-heavy, renders it still more unstable.

Viewed in this light the reversal of our economic policy means that, instead of concentrating our energies on the increase of supply while leaving demand to take care of itself, we should aim at maintaining a balance between demand and supply ; and the way to adjust this balance to-day is to advise people not to re-invest surplus wealth, but to spend it in the way it was the custom to spend it before the introduction of machinery and the limited liability company made possible constant reinvestment. To advise rich people to use their money in this way will doubtless appear to many to be a counsel of perfection which will not be listened to. But I am no pessimist in the matter. In the first place, because I believe a great proportion of the rich to-day reinvest rather than spend their money, not from any particular motive of gain, but because it is the custom ; and in the next, because the remainder will find after the war that the only way to secure themselves against personal violence is to use their money for the direct purpose of giving employment.

In the past surplus wealth was spent, among other things, upon the crafts and architecture, for building was never expected to pay. In this connection it may be interesting to quote the words of Pericles, who, in answer to some who complained that Athens was over-adorned like a woman wearing too many jewels, replied that surplus wealth was best spent upon such works as would bring eternal glory to the city and at the same time employ her artificers. I might add that many of the Greek Temples were built to find a solution to unemployed problems.

While at one end of the industrial scale our policy should be to get money spent freely on architecture and the crafts, thinking of architecture in the broadest sense as including all good building, at the other end agriculture should be revived. I feel little disposition to enlarge upon this issue, because I feel that it is going to be done, though perhaps from a different motive. Suffice it, however, to say that it is vital for the solution of our problems that the agricultural worker should be paid a wage equivalent to that of the industrial worker. Let us break for ever with the commercial tradition that useful work should be badly paid, for there is no more fruitful source of corruption in our midst than the knowledge that it is only by humbug and pretence that a man can escape from poverty.

It remains for me to thank the Editor of the *Daily Herald* for permission to reprint such of the articles as appeared in his journal, and the Editor of the *New Age* for permission to reprint part of this preface.

A. J. P.

66, STRAND ON GREEN, W 4

January 1917

CONTENTS

		PAGE
	PREFACE	7
I.	THE FABIAN COMPROMISE	23
II.	ON REASONING FROM FACT	30
III.	THE ECONOMIC, MORAL, AND POLITICAL CONTRA-DICTIONS OF COLLECTIVISM . . .	37
IV.	THE MEDIÆVAL GUILD SYSTEM . . .	44
V.	NATIONAL GUILDS AND THE GENERAL STRIKE .	50
VI.	THE ABOLITION OF THE WAGE SYSTEM . .	58
VII.	THE EVIL OF LARGE ORGANIZATIONS . .	65
VIII.	THE DIVISION OF LABOUR	74
IX.	MACHINERY AND INDUSTRY	82
X.	MACHINERY AND SOCIETY	89
XI.	THE ULTIMATE BASE OF INDUSTRIALISM . .	96
XII.	THE PLACE OF HANDICRAFT . . .	103
XIII.	THE ETHICS OF CONSUMPTION . . .	110

PAGE

XIV. THE TYRANNY OF THE MIDDLEMAN   .   . 117

XV. THE STRIKE FOR QUALITY 123

XVI. THE ELIMINATION OF THE MIDDLEMAN   .   . 130

XVII. THE DECENTRALIZATION OF INDUSTRY   . 135

XVIII. THE REDISTRIBUTION OF POPULATION   .   . 140

XIX. THE REABSORPTION OF THE PROFESSIONS   . 145

XX. THE TRADE DESIGNER   152

XXI. THE PROFESSION OF ARCHITECTURE   .   . 157

XXII. THE DESTRUCTIVE CONSUMPTION OF SURPLUS
      WEALTH   163

XXIII. ON PROPERTY   169

XXIV. THE LEISURE AND WORK STATES .   .   . 175

XXV. CONCLUSION 181

OLD WORLDS FOR NEW

I

THE FABIAN COMPROMISE

To one who is accustomed to view political activity from the somewhat detached and isolated standpoint of the social philosopher, there is something pathetic, not to say tragic, about the way Socialists are quarrelling among themselves to-day. And this not merely because capitalism is secure so long as they are content to consume their energies in mutual recrimination, but because Socialists themselves fail for the most part to discern clearly the root of the mischief. Abuse was at the beginning poured upon the Labour Party for its lack of courage and its inability to shape out an independent line of action. Nowadays,[1] those who acted more courageously are being made to suffer. It looks as if the experience of the French Revolution, when each group of reformers and enthusiasts was in turn supplanted by a group holding still more extreme views, is about to be repeated

[1] March 1914.

in miniature within the ranks of the Socialist movement. And it is possible that the reform movement to-day, like the French Revolution, may suffer a reaction.

Meanwhile, the most extraordinary thing in the whole situation is that few appear to have connected these quarrels with certain fundamental contradictions involved in Socialist theory. It is possible for a man to be consistent and courageous if he has behind him a consistent theory, but impossible if the theory be a bundle of contradictions. A man may not perceive such inconsistencies in theory, but he will, nevertheless, not escape being involved in them when he attempts to reduce them to practice. Such inconsistencies will paralyse his will, and a man who acted courageously at one time of his life will, to all appearances, tend to act like a coward at another. For when he is called upon to reduce such theories to practice, his policy will become involved in contradictions.

Such, it appears to me, has been the unfortunate fate of all our Socialist politicians, and I think we ought to be more generous in our criticisms of them. One and all find themselves in a false position to-day, and this not because of any particular moral delinquency, such as in our moments of disgust we are apt to ascribe to them, but because they have been committed to a theory which, to use an Americanism, " does not pan out." It will be my object in this and the succeeding articles to explain the nature of these contradictions of the Collectivist theory as a preliminary towards the formulation of a new Socialist policy.

On all sides we are being told to-day that Collectivism is dead. Superficially considered, in one sense that is true. The impossibility of creating a new social order purely by means of political action is widely realized. *Economic power precedes political power* is the new dogma to which nowadays we are asked to subscribe. Bureaucracy has been discovered to be a potential instrument of class oppression. Syndicalism and National Guilds are united in demanding the right of the producer to a share in the control of industry as opposed to control by the consumer, which was the faith of Collectivism. But that is as far as things have gone. Fundamentally most Socialists are Collectivists still. They have not yet thrown overboard its philosophy, and not until it is repudiated root and branch can there be any hope of the growth of Socialist unity. In a word, Collectivism as an immediate policy is now fortunately discredited, but as a philosophy it survives subconsciously in thought, and for that reason it still controls the destinies of the movement.

To understand any such theory as Collectivism it is necessary in the first place to understand exactly the circumstances which brought it into existence. We have moved so far away from the thoughts of the 'eighties that it is difficult for us to realize what ideas it sought to supplant.

In those days almost everybody believed in competition as the only safeguard against monopoly. The rights of the individual and of property took precedence of the rights of the community. In fact, the idea that the community might have a corporate life was non-existent. The Collectivist theory was gradually evolved from the necessity of combating such ways of thinking rather than from the fundamental needs of social reconstruction. In the early days of the Socialist movement there was a great struggle between William Morris and Mr. Sidney Webb and their supporters in respect to the policy to be pursued. Morris was undoubtedly right in the position he took up, because he went back to the fundamental needs of human nature. Mr. Webb, however, triumphed within the movement because he was more practical in the immediate sense, though, as I shall show later, he was fundamentally unsound. He perceived more clearly than Morris the immediate work which might be done. He compromised with things as they are, and he could do this because he was blind to certain defects of the present system. Morris saw in industrialism a great ugly fact which produced shoddy goods and sweated the workers, and he knew that these things had a common cause. Mr. Webb, on the other hand, without the fine æsthetic perceptions of Morris, saw only the sweated workers. He thought he could find a remedy for sweating as a separate and detached issue and accepted industrialism as an established fact in the belief that it might be humanized. He was successful within the movement because the majority had not then begun to suspect industrialism, for the gulf which separated Morris from the masses was in his day too wide to be bridged. Before that was possible much spade-work had to be done, and the theory of Collectivism as evolved by Mr. Webb proved to be the only available instrument for the purpose.

What we are witnessing to-day in the confusion in which the Socialist movement is involved is the break-up of this compromise, first in regard to policy, and second in regard to theory. When the Labour Party arrived at the House of Commons, great things were expected from it. Disappointment followed. The reason is, as I have already pointed out, that they were in a false position and committed to an impossible theory. That theory in turn is now being exploded. I will not refer to the Syndicalist and National Guilds propaganda, which have assailed it from without, for we now have evidence that it has utterly broken down from within. The last two years the Fabian Society has been engaged in collecting data for a report on the control of industry. Last month[1] the *New Statesman* published the draft of the first part of the report written for the Research Committee by Mr. and Mrs. Sidney Webb, as

[1] *The Control of Industry*, *New Statesman* Special Supplement, February 14, 1914.

a special supplement. We find there what many of us expected—a proposal to reorganize industry on a basis of "speeding-up." Of course it is not called "speeding-up." Mr. and Mrs. Webb are more diplomatic than that. They call it "efficiency" and "discipline," but there is no mistaking their meaning. Criticizing the Nelson Self-Help Manufacturing Society, they say, in respect to the comparatively low output of the society, that "in private factories, failure to produce the average is followed by dismissal. In this society the workers, feeling assured that no such course will be followed, work easily, pay no regard to the possibility of a division of profits if greater effort were to be put forth, regard themselves as having a job for life, and take their work in a leisurely fashion."

Reading this, we are not surprised to find that their sympathies are entirely with the Co-operative Productive Societies, where "speeding-up" evidently obtains. For, they tell us, "these societies, having become attached as subordinate adjuncts to Co-operative Societies of Consumers, are not subject to the special drawbacks of Associations of Producers, inasmuch as the Co-operative Societies of Consumers furnish all the capital required and supply a Committee of Management who do not work in the workshops. They govern, and thus the manager finds in the committee the support he needs for the maintenance of discipline." There is no more to be said ! Collectivism is bankrupt. It never presumed to be an artistic ideal. It has ended in not even daring to be a human one. The Anti-Socialist who told us that Socialism left human nature out of account stands justified. Mr. and Mrs. Webb evidently support him. If this report is to become the democratic programme of the future, the movement will have to take down its banner on which is inscribed "Government of the people, by the people, for the people," and put in its place "Exploitation of the people, by the people, for the people." For this, in substance, is what the report recommends.

II

ON REASONING FROM FACT

I HAVE drawn attention to the bankruptcy in which Collectivist theory finds itself nowadays, and showed how, commencing with a compromise with industrialism, it has ended in a shameless advocacy of the reorganization of industry on a basis of "speeding-up." There are certain interesting questions which arise immediately out of this miscarriage, which I now propose to discuss.

Now it is in the first place to be observed that although Mr. and Mrs. Webb endorse "speeding-up" in their report on the control of industry, if rumour is to be credited, there is little chance of the report being adopted by the Fabian Society. Whatever the faults of the Fabian may be, he is, generally speaking, a humane person, and when a clear and definite issue presents itself, as it does in this case, as to whether Socialists should or should not approve of "speeding-up" in industry, there can be little doubt as to which way his opinion will go. I do not believe that the gentle persuasiveness of Mr. Webb will prevail against the sentiment of the society on this occasion. All the same, Mr. Webb has reason on his side. What he recommends may be inhuman, but it is the logical deduction from Collectivist doctrine, and the Fabian Society must find itself in the position of either adopting this report or repudiating the theory of Collectivism. This is, of course, if logic is to prevail ; for if it be true, as Collectivists affirm, that the evolution which is taking place in industry is from a lower to a higher plane of perfection, then it follows logically that the phenomenon which accompanies such a transition is justifiable. I can see no escape from this dilemma for such as accept the Collectivist position. To quote a popular phrase, "You can't eat your cake and have it."

It is not necessary for me to review all the arguments by which Mr. Belloc showed that the trend of modern legislation, based upon Collectivist ideas, is towards the establishment of the Servile State. Only Servile Socialists, who are destitute alike of the sense of liberty and human dignity, will be found to deny it. The point which I wish to make here is that we shall not escape from this fate merely by protesting against it. If we are to ward off the Servile State, it will be necessary for us to understand exactly the nature of the forces which are alluring us to our enslavement. To grapple with these forces we shall have to relinquish many prejudices, for it is upon our prejudices that

the Servile State is being built. Foremost
among them is the prejudice of the modern
intellectual against all reasoning which is not
based upon material facts. It is a stupid
prejudice, because it has this important defect
—that it is impossible with this mental attitude
to be wise before the event ; for it is not until
after the event that the facts are available to
reason upon. People who are wise before the
event reason from a metaphysical position and
a knowledge of human nature. This is natural,
because it is the spirit of man which is the
creative force in society and is the cause of
things. Phenomena are the manifestation of the
spirit in the material universe. To base our
reasoning on social questions entirely upon
phenomena, which alone in these days are
recognized as facts, is to leave out of our
calculations the most important facts of life. The
facts of human nature are not to be weighed
and measured by Fabian investigators, and yet
they are ultimately the only facts that matter,
for the good will of men is necessary to the
smooth working of any social system. By
reasoning based exclusively upon industrial
phenomena, it is possible for Mr. Webb to arrive
at the conclusion that " speeding-up " is a
necessary stage of economic development. He
reckons, however, without human nature when he
expects men to submit to such a tyranny without
protest ; for a point is reached in the development of tyranny when men will remain quiescent

no longer. A spirit of restlessness is engendered which at any moment may break loose in open rebellion and upset purely economic calculations. For man has a soul which craves satisfaction, and refuses obedience to a system whose only aim is to make cotton and buttons as cheaply as possible.

Of course it is easy to understand why Fabianism should have degenerated in this way. In its anxiety to find an immediate remedy for the problems of poverty it ignored the claims of art and philosophy, not understanding that every practical problem has a metaphysical problem behind it, and that the needs of art in industry are identical with the needs of human nature. Further, it is to some extent to be explained by the artificial lives which members of the Fabian Society lead. Mr. Webb is typical. At first as a Civil servant, and then as a man of private means, he has lived a sheltered life far removed from the storm and stress of things, while his legal training was the very worst imaginable for intensifying in him sympathies which were never too strong. And so with respect to the Fabian Society as a whole ; it is far too intellectual and too little human ever to get at grips with the realities of life, while the occupations of its members are for the most part of too artificial a nature to give them a fund of first-hand experience. To be candid, the Fabians are the last people in this world to find a remedy for the evils which afflict society.   They are too much a part of the same disease.

Now it is to be observed that whether a man understands human nature or not, he cannot with safety leave it outside his calculations.   The difference between the Fabian and the mystic is not that the Fabian has an eye on facts, and the mystic has not, but that the Fabian sees only the material fact while the mystic sees its spiritual significance.   In other words, the mystic sees the exact relation each separate fact bears to the moral as well as to the material universe. This arises, of course, from the circumstance that the mystic is not only intensely human himself, but knows the science of human nature, which is what we understand by a metaphysical position. The mystic, because of this knowledge, interprets facts in a different light—in the light of that higher unity which alone can reconcile apparent contradictions.   In practice he will differ from the Fabian in this way—that he will not seek to establish principles by the mere aggregation of facts.   He knows that really fundamental principles are not to be discovered in this way. On the other hand, he perceives in every fact the workings of a universal principle.   Like Blake, he feels—

> A dog starved at its master's gate
> Predicts the ruin of the State.

The reason why he knows this is because at the back of his mind there is a conception of order, which enables him to distinguish clearly between what is an accidental and what is a permanent factor in human affairs. The Fabian, on the other hand, not finding this order within himself, and yet at the same time feeling the need of order, seeks to discover certainty in the external order of phenomena. Being without exact standards of truth, goodness, and beauty, he comes to accept as standards such things as speed, bigness, quantity, and success, which henceforth he regards as the touchstones of "efficiency." The mystic knows all this to be pure illusion and the Fabian finds it out too ; for he tends daily to become more and more of an opportunist, and to settle each question as it arises without regard to wider issues ; only to find his predictions falsified at a later date.

.   .   .   .   /   .

In *The Comments of Bagshot* are some observations on the influence of statistics, which are interesting to quote in this connection.

Statistics are the clinical thermometers of the modern world. There is an incessant taking of temperatures, followed by jealous comparison of the resulting records, and every patient examines not only his own but every other patient's fever chart. This is a chronic source of jealousy and unrest in the modern world. It tends at times to an almost insane hypochondria, in which the patient declares himself ill beyond recovery, though his appetite is enormous and his growth increasing.

The habit encouraged by statisticians of weighing quantities, instead of measuring qualities, is most debasing to ideals in a modern State. It is habitually taken for granted that a nation must be inferior to its rivals if it falls short of them in population, territory, or volume of trade. . . . Of what use is it to cry out on the vulgarity of worshipping wealth, when all the great nations and their statesmen and spokesmen deliberately preach to us that the richest among them is the greatest ? The chief need of Europe to-day is to recover the thought that a country may hold the primacy of the world by leading it in ideas and the art of living. But we shall not do that till we have shut half the Government departments and killed all the statisticians.[1]

---

[1] *Comments of Bagshot*, by J. A. Spender.

III

THE ECONOMIC, MORAL, AND POLITICAL CONTRADICTIONS OF COLLECTIVISM

CONSIDERING the confusion of thought in which, at the latter end of the nineteenth century, art and philosophy were enveloped, there was certainly some excuse for the Fabian Society in disregarding their claims. But it is different with regard to morals. When we remember that twenty years before the Fabian Essays were written, Ruskin had exposed the fallacies inherent in the divorce of economics from morals, it is difficult to absolve Fabians from the charge of stupidity in imagining that they could afford to ignore his teachings. Yet, strange as this may seem, it is stranger still that they should have to this day continued in the error, when we remember that from the very start it has been behind the frequent quarrels and splits in the Socialist movement. The split over the Boer War provides a convenient illustration.

It will be remembered that the Boer War led to serious divisions within the ranks of the Socialist movement. The Independent Labour Party and Social Democratic Federation were resolute in their opposition to it. But the Fabian Society temporized for a long time, and after a split, when many resigned their membership, the Executive issued a manifesto in the form of a booklet by Mr. Bernard Shaw entitled *Fabianism and the Empire*. In it the divorce between Collectivist economics and Socialist morals first saw the clear light of day. In this manifesto Mr. Shaw did not discuss the moral aspects of the war. The right and wrong of the question did not concern him. He accepted the war as an established fact or a necessary evil. Small nationalities were a nuisance, and had always been a source of trouble and difficulty. A United South Africa under the British Flag, he told us, was the only possible policy to support. That such a union should be brought about by the sinister power of capitalism did not concern him, as he imagined it would be a stepping-stone to the Socialist millennium.

We know to-day that such is not the case. A United South African Government is now an established fact, but the racial troubles have not been moderated.[1] Indeed, they seem to be only just beginning. What the upshot will be of all

---

[1] It will be remembered that in February 1914 there was a great strike in the Rand, which was terminated by the action of General Smuts, who deported the labour leaders and brought the Boer farmers into the towns to fire upon the miners.

that is taking place there nowadays God alone knows. Of one thing, however, we may be sure —that the war has not simplified the problem, and that with the triumph of capitalism the Socialist millennium is not any nearer. All the same, according to Collectivist economics, Mr. Bernard Shaw and the Fabians who supported him were in the right, and the Independent Labour Party and Social Democratic Federation abanr doned their claims to be Collectivist bodies in opposing the war. For Collectivism is an economic theory, and we are told economics have nothing to do with morals. Yet, strange to say, Socialists who saw the Boer War as a capitalist war, and as something inimical to the interests of Labour, nevertheless failed to see the evil inherent in the growth of capitalism when war was not in question. I remember at the time listening to the conversation of a leading member of the Independent Labour Party, deploring the war in one breath and in the other rejoicing in the doings of the late Mr. Pierpont Morgan, who at the time had just organized the Steel Trust of America and was attempting the trustification of transatlantic shipping. Mr. Morgan, he said, was paving the way to the Socialist State. Of course, in one sense that is true. The growth of capitalism is making men think and is creating the spirit of rebellion ; but, needless to say, that is not the sense in which our Independent Labour Party member meant it.

I said that Collectivism is an economic theory

divorced from morals. This is its central weakness, because in practice it is impossible to disregard moral issues without feeling a bit of a cad. The ordinary decent man will always decline to pursue a course of action which is morally culpable. And the ordinary man is right. In so far as economic considerations have become divorced from morals, they are only an encumbrance to right action. Two men in the Socialist movement, and two only—Mr. Sidney Webb and Mr. Bernard Shaw—have sufficiently transcended ordinary human limitations, and have been able to base their actions upon economic theory in an entirely disinterested way. The ordinary mortal, when he bases his action upon economic theory, is apt to be on the make. Hence it is that a social theory deduced entirely from a study of economic phenomena can in practice only exist to confuse the issue. Here we have the source of the confusion which has followed on the trail of the Labour Party ever since it entered Parliament. No issue which has ever come along has been for it a clear issue between right and wrong. The economic theory to which it subscribes has always blinded it to the rights and wrongs of the issues which confronted it. The triumph of Collectivist theory placed Socialists entirely in the hands of capitalists. They agreed with the big capitalists because on economic theory they had no reason to disagree. The capitalist finds in Collectivist doctrine justification for his actions. What theory could be more acceptable to him than one which tells him that sweating is not his concern and can only be remedied by the State ; and that in so far as he can succeed in ruining his competitor, he is but the natural agent of an economic evolution which is leading to the millennium?   Can we wonder that he should seek to shuffle his responsibility on to the shoulders of the State, when we remember that Collectivism seeks to exonerate him from all personal responsibility?

The Collectivist idea of holding the State responsible for all the ills of society has been another source of confusion.   For it is apparent that the State cannot, in the long run, be better than the citizens who compose it.   To hold the State responsible is finally to hold no one responsible, because the politicians themselves, who at any time form the Government, are only in possession of a delegated authority.   In a far higher degree than capitalists they are the creatures of circumstances.   They do not control the State, but the State controls them.   By this I mean that they are at the mercy of the bureaucratic departments and their permanent officials, for, as Sir John Gorst said, by the time a Minister has got the hang of things in his department his term of office is nearing its close.   In the State departments no one feels any particular sense of personal responsibility, because of the divided responsibility which obtains there, which has come into existence for the very purpose of preventing any particular individual from exercising too much authority. If politicians are to act at all, they can only do so to-day by availing themselves of the services of this unwieldy and impersonal machinery, which proceeds automatically, according to the laws of its own growth, and which bears no particular relationship to the thoughts and feelings of those who form a part of it.

The Insurance Act will for all time remain the classical example of the failure necessarily following any attempt at reform by wholesale measures. Mr. Lloyd George is in these days a much-abused man.[1] But Collectivists have no right to criticize him, for all that he did was to attempt to give practical application to principles which they had popularized. With the Socialist agitation at one side of him demanding that something should be done, and capitalism at the other as determined as ever to exploit men, it is not surprising that he failed, for failure must be the inevitable destination of reformers who imagine they can find a remedy for the evils of poverty by compromising with things as they are. I do not believe that the Act was framed by Mr. George for the oppression of the poor, but that such is its result in practice admits of no question.

The underlying cause of all this confusion, in the words of a French Syndicalist, is that " you cannot at the same time fight the enemy and co-operate with him." It is a mistake for reformers to have any dealings with the State until such

[1] Needless to say, this was written before the war.

time arrives as they are capable of bargaining with it on equal terms. Meanwhile the best policy to pursue is so to consolidate our forces, so to clarify our minds, that when we do act we shall be able to do so with certainty and precision ; and the first step towards this consummation is such a thorough overhauling of Socialist theory as will banish for ever the contradictions involved in its moral, economic, and political theories.

IV

THE MEDIÆVAL GUILD SYSTEM

AFTER explaining the nature of the economic, moral, and political confusion which followed the acceptance by Socialists of Collectivist economics, I concluded the last article by saying that our immediate need is such a thorough overhauling of Socialist theory as will banish for ever these contradictions. With an understanding of the underlying principles of the Mediæval Guild System, we shall be in a better position to face the modern problems. All clear thinking pre-supposes some clear and definable standards of thought. Just in the same way that definite conceptions of the nature of truth, goodness, and beauty are necessary to clear reasoning, so the Guilds serve the purpose of a standard to guide us in our elucidation of the problems of social reorganization.

What, then, is the Guild System? It is the system under which industry at all times was organized, wherever men were free to co-operate together. In Western Europe the Guilds existed until the close of the Middle Ages. They fell

before the economic and political upheavals which
accompanied the discovery of America and the
sea route to Asia, which involved as a natural
consequence the change of trade routes and the
growth of capitalism.   In Asia the Guilds have
continued down to this day, though they are
suffering from European competition.   In India
they are in a state of disintegration ; their integrity having been undermined by the British
Government, which deprived them of their
privileges in the interests of Lancashire manu-
facturers.

The idea which underlay the Guild System was
that men should be organized in groups, and
that the State existed to facilitate their co-operation.   In the sphere of industry the natural division
was that of trades.   Each trade had its own Guild,
and every craftsman was obliged to become a
member of it.   The Guild had a monopoly of
its trade, and exercised a jurisdiction over its
members, which was delegated to it by State
and municipality.   The Guild was a centre of
mutual aid ; it gave assistance to the sick and
unfortunate ; it regulated wages and hours of
labour ; fixed prices and the quality of work
done ; fixed the training of apprentices and
limited the number of men any master might
employ.   The Cloth Weavers Guild of Flanders,
which was typical of many, only allowed three
journeymen to each master.

There is an interesting description of Guilds
in the building trade given by Professor Lethaby

in a lecture on "Technical Education in the
Building Trades." It runs :—

In the Middle Ages, the Masons' and Carpenters' Guilds
were faculties or colleges of education in those arts, and
every town was, so to say, a craft university. Corporations
of Masons, Carpenters, and the like were established in the
towns ; each craft aspired to have a college hall. The
universities themselves have been well named by a recent
historian "Scholars' Guilds." The Guild, which recognized
all the customs of its trade, guaranteed the relations of the
apprentice and master craftsman with whom he was placed ;
but he was really apprenticed to the craft as a whole, and
ultimately to the city, whose freedom he engaged to take up.
He was, in fact, a graduate of his craft college and wore its
robes. At a later stage the apprentice became a companion
or bachelor of his art, or by producing a master-work, the
thesis of his craft, he was admitted a master. Only then was
he permitted to become an employer of labour, or was admitted as one of the governing body of his college. As a
citizen, city dignities were open to him. He might become
the master in building some abbey or cathedral, or, as King's
mason, become a member of the royal household, the ac-
knowledged great master of his time in mason-craft. With
such a system, was it so very wonderful that the buildings of
the Middle Ages, which were indeed wonderful, should have
been produced?

Considerations of space will not allow me to
enter more into the details of the Guilds, and there
is no reason why I should. What I have already
said is sufficient for the purpose of familiarizing
the reader with the idea of the Guilds. If he
is interested in the subject he can read up about
them for himself, and, in this connection, there
are two books which I would particularly recom-

mend. One of them is *Mutual Aid*, by Prince Kropotkin, and the other is *The Indian Craftsman*, by Dr. Ananda K. Coomaraswamy. Both of them are extremely able. Dr. Coomaraswamy's book is especially interesting, as he describes the Indian Guilds which are still in existence, though, as I have already said, they are in a state of decline. It is satisfactory, however, to learn that of late years a movement has arisen in India to preserve them. Prince Kropotkin's book is, fortunately, well known to Socialists, and needs no words of recommendation from me.

Two functions engaged the activities of the Guilds. One of them was that of mutual aid ; the other was the safeguarding of the standard of production against commercial abuses. The first of these functions is nowadays undertaken by the Trades Unions, though the Guilds, being wealthy bodies, were able to be much more generous in the assistance they gave to their members. In fact, the Guilds fulfilled for their members those functions which are now undertaken by the Poor Law, only they were undertaken in a different spirit. This was notably the case in the treatment of widows and orphans, who were provided for out of the funds of the Guild, and that in a manner befitting their station in life, not in the despicably niggardly way which is customary with Boards of Guardians. This came about naturally, it is to be supposed, because when men are organized in localized groups they are held together by personal and human ties,

which are real bonds ; whereas the Poor Law
is, at the best, a piece of impersonal machinery
for assisting those who have no personal claim
upon us, but only on the community ; and it is
not easy for the average person to act as generously
towards strangers as towards his own kith and
kin.

The other function of the Guilds was the protection of the standard in production. With that
fine instinct for sociological truth which is characteristic of all early societies, the Mediævalists
recognized that the best way to protect the
standard of life of the craftsman was ultimately
to protect the standard of quality in craftsmanship.
This is the vitalizing principle of the Guilds as
industrial organizations, and it is only by relating
all their regulations to this central idea that they
can be properly understood.   To protect the
standard of craftsmanship, it was necessary, before
everything else, that the craftsman should be privileged ; for privilege not only protected him from
the competition of unscrupulous rivals, but it also
secured him leisure in his work.   Both of these
conditions are necessary for the production of good
work.   Unless a man can work leisurely, it is
impossible for him to put his best thought into
his work, and unless a man is protected from
the competition of unscrupulous rivals, who undercut him in price and jerry their work in the
unseen parts, it is impossible for him to remain
a conscientious producer. Experience has proved
that the public, as consumers, cannot be relied

upon to check that gradual deterioration in the quality of wares which is the inevitable accompaniment of unfettered individual competition. Privilege and protection are the corner-stones of production for use and beauty, just as much as commercialism and competition are the corner-stones of production for profit. The fundamental difference between the Mediæval and modern polity is that, whereas the modern aims at the abolition of all privilege, the Mediævalist sought to secure privileges for all. It is the difference between pulling down and building up.

Finally, it is necessary for me to controvert one objection which is often made to the restoration of the Guilds. In order to justify the present age, it has been the custom of modernists to misrepresent the past. The consequence is that in the popular mind the Middle Ages has become synonymous with Feudalism, and even then, not Feudalism as it really existed—for in contrast with capitalism, Feudalism was a comparatively humane institution—but misrepresented out of all resemblance to the original. It is not my purpose to defend Feudalism, but merely to point out that Feudalism was all along at enmity with the Guilds and Mediæval cities, and in the struggle the Guilds were worsted. Their destruction was the destruction of real democracy. And the best testimony I can bring in support of this contention is that of Kropotkin, who says that " most of what the Socialist aims at existed in the Mediæval city."

V

NATIONAL GUILDS AND THE GENERAL STRIKE

THE brief account I have given of the Mediæval Guild System will help us in a consideration of the proposals of the *New Age* for its restoration. The articles of the Guild writers were originally advanced under the name of Guild Socialism. Latterly their scheme has been re-named "National Guilds," which, I think, is a pity. Guild Socialism is a better rallying cry.

The *New Age* proposals are shortly as follows : The workers are advised to fuse all the Unions connected with each separate industry into huge national organizations ; and then, after getting all the workers, including the salariat, to become members of these Unions, they should create Labour monopolies within each industry. When any Union has by this means become blackleg-proof, the workers are urged to demand not merely higher wages, but superior status ; by which is meant, that the workers would cease to sell their labour as a commodity in the market, and become partners in the direction and control of industry.

Should the capitalists refuse this demand, then a strike would be declared. The Unions being thus in a position to hold up industry, and with the intelligent public on their side, the State would find it necessary to step in. It would buy out the capitalists by offering them a reasonable sum or by guaranteeing them an income for a period of years, retain nominal possession of the so-acquired capital, charter the Union (now become a Guild by the inclusion of the salariat), which would henceforth carry on the industry on terms mutually fair and favourable. The Guild, in return for this charter guaranteeing it privileges of national monopoly and self-government, would undertake certain responsibilities relating to the quality and quantity of goods produced—and also on behalf of its own members, other Guilds, the public at large, and the State itself. This proposal is supported by an economic theory called " The Abolition of the Wage System," which I shall consider later.

Needless to say, I am in perfect accord with the general idea of restoring the Guilds. The thanks of the Socialist movement are due to the *New Age* for the valuable work it has done in securing recognition for the Guild principle as the basis of political, social, and industrial reorganization. If democracy is ever to achieve self-expression, it can only be by men organizing themselves into groups. Parliamentary democracy as it exists to-day has no organic structure. It is merely an aggregation of people who unite for some one to represent them in respect to issues which are not of their making. The issues are so confused that it is almost impossible for the ordinary man, who is not in possession of inside knowledge, to get the hang of them ; while, if he could, he would not be much better off, because they are not the real issues. In order, therefore, to create the real issues, it becomes necessary to break up this aggregation by organizing men into groups. The natural divisions of such groupings of men are by trades. Though the average man is apt to talk nonsense about national politics, he can generally talk sense about his own trade or occupation. The reason for this is because the issues are fewer and he is quite familiar with them. Hence, the re-organization of democracy on the Mediæval basis can be fruitful only of good results. Guild democracy, I am persuaded, is the only real democracy, and if ever democracy is to reflect the general will of the community and to free itself from the machinations of politicians, it will need to revive the Guilds.

So far so good. It is when we pass on from a consideration of the end to be attained to the means of bringing that end about that I am inclined to question the wisdom of the *New Age* proposals. Working upon their lines, I do not think it will be possible for the State to secure possession of the capital in industry, apart from the will of the capitalists. For the State is the capitalists. I fear that if the State should take

over the railways, and should take the workers
into partnership, which is extremely improbable,
that it would be on terms favourable to the
capitalists, and because it suited their convenience.
The wealthy would receive their dividends as
hitherto, but guaranteed by the State ; while the
control given to the workers would only be
nominal. They would not be allowed a say in
the things that really mattered. So again with
respect to the policy of strikes, which are relied
upon to bring capitalism to its knees, I doubt
the possibility of getting the workers, under normal
circumstances, to strike for superior status, and
it appears to be the opinion also of men who have
had practical experience of organizing strikes.
Men can be induced to strike for higher wages,
for shorter hours, against some tyranny, or to
see justice done to a pal, but not for status.
That is one of the results of the wage-system.
The average working man to-day is too down-
trodden to believe he might be successful in demanding such a change. His immediate need
is for higher wages and shorter hours. These
are things which, to him, are definite and tangible.
And, in striking for them, he feels he has a
sporting chance of success. But superior status
is a different matter. It is a remote issue, and,
under normal circumstances, it is to be feared
he would not entertain the idea of claiming it.
Before it would be possible for the workers to
make such a demand, their spirits would have
to be raised. They would need to be drunk

with enthusiasm, such as might possibly be the case in the event of a general strike, when the spirits of the individual worker would be sustained by the spirit of enthusiasm and rebellion which pervaded the whole community. I feel justified, therefore, in associating the *New Age* policy of restoring the Guilds with the idea of the general strike.

What, then, are the prospects of changing the basis of society, and restoring the Guilds by means of a general strike? My opinion is that our chances of success are not great. The failure of the general strike in Sweden is not encouraging. Moreover, the difficulty of controlling any policy based upon strikes is very great. When men are successful in a strike, they are apt to overestimate their power and to bring about reaction. The success of the Dock Strike of 1911 was due to the fact that the masters were unprepared, the failure of the one in 1912 because they were ready. How much greater would be this difficulty after a general upheaval it is impossible to say. Men, when they are flushed with success, are not inclined to listen to the counsels of moderation, and without moderation they would certainly be finally beaten. There is also a further difficulty. The workers are not to-day united by a common economic bond. There is the same division of interests between them as there was between the serfs and retainers of the Feudal Lords. In our society, probably half of the working class are parasitic upon the rich, in the sense that they are employed by them, either in personal service or in the manufacture of articles which only the rich can afford to buy. Mr. Bernard Shaw discussed the problem which this class of workers presented some years ago in a series of articles entitled " The Parasitic Proletariat " which he contributed to the *New Age*. He could find no solution, though he sought by economic abstractions to show that the interests of the parasitic proletariat and the proletariat proper are ultimately identical. But such abstractions are of no assistance to us when dealing with concrete issues ; for in times of crisis it is the immediate interest, rather than the ultimate one, which decides things. If the workers did succeed in a general strike, their success could only be temporary. To make it permanent they would need to deal promptly with this parasitic proletariat, whose market would be gone with the disappearance of the rich. This, I feel, would be impossible amid the general confusion which would certainly obtain. Revolution would be followed by a counter-revolution. The parasitic proletariat would rally to the support of the wealthy in order to recover a market for their work.

Yet I believe a revolution will come. Sooner or later it will be forced upon us by the problem of over-production. When machinery was first introduced, England had the whole world in which to dispose of its surplus products. But no nation can afford to be a consumer of machine-produced goods permanently. The suction would drain its economic resources. Hence it has happened that one after another of the nations which were once our customers have been drawn into the vicious circle of commercial production, and have become our competitors for markets. We are rapidly approaching a time when there will be no new markets left to exploit. What is going to happen when that limit is reached? Surely it can only be economic collapse. Karl Marx was right in foreseeing this catastrophic ending of quantitative machine-production. Where he was wrong was in supposing that out of the unemployed a revolutionary force could be created. Unemployed men cannot rebel, for they have no economic, political, military, or moral power. They are simply demoralized men, who are thankful for a meal. It is dangerous to prophesy, but it is my opinion, and I give it for what it is worth, that when a revolution does come, it will come from above and not from below. It may come as a result of war, as was the case with the Russian Revolution, which followed the war with Japan, or by a division in the governing class, as was the case in the French Revolution, or by a combination of both circumstances. War seems to me the more probable because, when new markets are exhausted, the governing class will be driven into it in order to safeguard their own position. But they will probably fail.[1]

---

[1] Looking at this issue from the standpoint of to-day, there is a sense in which Karl Marx may be said to have been right.

Meanwhile it is well to remember that revolution is a purely destructive force. Just as the French Revolution broke the power of Feudalism, and liberated the bourgeois, so the coming revolution will break the power of capitalism and liberate forces which are germinating in our midst. It is for us to educate these forces ; to see that the people know which are the real issues and can distinguish between the true and the false. If they are able to do so, then reconstruction will be rapid ; if not, a period of anarchy may ensue.

The prodigious dimensions of the unemployed problem after the war may be such as to precipitate not only revolution but the end of capitalist domination. For it is not to be expected that a class which to-day fails to appreciate the economic significance of the war even to the extent of realizing that the limits of industrial expansion have been reached, will be able to cope successfully with after-the-war problems.

VI

THE ABOLITION OF THE WAGE SYSTEM

In the last chapter I considered the *New Age* proposal which has been advanced under the name of " National Guilds " in its relation to the general strike. In this one I propose to discuss the theory of " The Abolition of the Wage System," by which the Guild writers seek to give economic justification for their proposals. It is not a new theory, as it finds a place in the economic analysis of Karl Marx, but by its association with the idea of restoring the Guilds it has acquired a new significance. In bringing together the two ideas the Guild writers have strengthened the case for each : they are, indeed, related as the body and the soul.

What, then, is meant by the demand for the abolition of the wage system? It is that in the future labour shall not be treated as a commodity to be bought by capitalists at the current market rate in the same way that goods and raw materials are bought ; that the income of the workers shall not be dependent upon the variations of supply and demand ; and that men are not to be only employed when it suits the convenience of capitalists, and turned adrift to starve when he can make no profit out of their labour. Also, it is a demand that the workers shall have status and receive pay instead of wages, the difference between pay and wages being that men who receive pay, as do soldiers or civil servants, receive a fixed income, whereas wages as paid to the labourer are not continuous in this way, but subject to breaks during unemployment.

Now, just in the same way that I find myself in agreement with the Guild writers, in respect to the general idea of restoring the Guilds, and yet differ from them in regard to policy, so I find similar grounds of agreement and disagreement when I consider the economic theory of the abolition of the wage system. The reason for my disagreement is this : That they seem to regard the institution of wages as an absolute evil, whereas, in my opinion, it is only relative. Under the Mediæval Guild system the journeymen and apprentices received what were, technically speaking, wages ; but they did not suffer from the evils which we associate with the wage system to-day, because masters and men were alike members of the same Guilds, and were bound together by personal and human ties. Though wages existed under the Guild system, they did not imply the brutal and inhuman relationship which they do to-day. For labour

was not then a commodity, the price of which
was determined by the competition of the market,
but was paid for at a fixed rate, determined
by the Guilds. Moreover, the journeyman only
remained a wage-earner during the earlier part
of his life. He could look forward to setting
up in business on his own account, as a matter
of course, for as there was a limit placed to
the number of assistants that any man could
employ, opportunities for advancement were
opened to all who desired to use them. The
wage system, therefore, did not in those days
present itself as an evil in the way it does
to-day.[1] It is the growth of large organizations, the system of the division of labour, and
the ever-extending use of machinery that has
created the evils which we associate with the
wage system, for under a system of large
organizations those personal relationships which
humanize life tend to disappear, and their place
is taken by a cash-nexus divorced from all
sentiment and personal regard. It is this which
makes the wage system to-day so brutal, and
why we must raise our voices in protest against
it. But I am persuaded that our efforts will be
misdirected and fruitless if we merely demand
its abolition. We shall miss our central aim,
which is to humanize the relations of society ;

[1] The Statute of Apprentices passed in 1563, which sought to
establish by law Trade Guild custom, enacted that journeymen
must be retained in service at least one year, and must receive
three months' notice of a coming dismissal.

for pay may be substituted for wages, and yet the relations of men may be anything but human.

There is another reason why we should work along these lines. The central weakness of any attempt to abolish the wage system by taking the citadel of capitalism by storm is that it is precisely those trades and occupations that suffer most from the evils of the wage system which are least able to offer effective resistance to it. Railwaymen, it is true, get wages, but their work is so regular that in most cases they may be almost said to be in receipt of pay. But with the workers in the building trades it is different. Their work is intermittent, and it is difficult to see how it could be otherwise. All building jobs come to an end sooner or later. It would be futile, therefore, for the workers in the building trades to demand pay instead of wages, for they would be demanding something which the employers would be powerless to give. The building trade employers are not like the railway companies, in a secure position and able to levy tribute on the people, but are dependent for their work on a demand which is erratic and impossible to gauge. To some extent they are in exactly the same position as the men, inasmuch as, like them, they are constantly in the position of having to look around for new sources of work. In a word, the employers of the building trades could not give the workers status, because they have not got status themselves.

Looking, then, at the problem of the building

trades—and from this point of view it is, indeed, typical of an enormous number of other trades— it is apparent that before the workers could possibly find themselves in a position to demand status it will be necessary to take measures to regularize demand. In the Minority Report of the Poor Law Commission, Mr. and Mrs. Webb ran up against this problem, and recommended the establishment of a Central Bureau to attempt the regularization of demand for public works. In this limited sphere such an arrangement might do good, but it is obviously impossible to give application to such arrangements on a national scale, because the factors underlying industrial instability are too many to be controlled from without. If this problem is to be solved at all, it will only be by attacking it at its roots, which we find to be in the instability of our tastes, the uncertainty of our aims and the confusion of our thoughts. These are the things which give rise to irregularity of employment, in so far as it is not due to changing climatic conditions and other natural causes. It will be by seeking to bring order into them that we shall gradually bring order into our social arrangements ; which problem, I would add incidentally, we shall never solve until we learn to respect the wisdom of the artist and the philosopher : it is the key to the whole situation.

A common source of our confusion is that in our schemes for the reorganization of society we fail to distinguish clearly between two fundamentally different types of industry which might be termed respectively the "constants" and the "variables." The distinction has always, to some extent, existed, but in modern industry the "constants" have become more constant and the "variables" more variable. Latter-day schemes of reform would accentuate these differences. They always assume that it is possible to make the variables constant by means of external arrangements. To my way of thinking this is impossible, as it is not in the nature of things, and every effort to make one section of industry more constant by regulations can only result in increasing the variability of what remains.

If I have questioned the wisdom of the *New Age* proposals, it has not been without a deep sense of obligation to them for the issues they have raised. As a generalization there is this to be said for the *New Age* theory : that it has focussed attention on the central evils of modern society. Collectivism insisted too much on the relation of man to his environment : it forgot the relationship in which man stands to man. The theory of " the abolition of the wage system " has raised this central issue. In a perfect society every man would be in the right place, for men can only co-operate successfully together when each man performs the function for which by Nature he is the most perfectly fitted. It is the eternal problem of society to find ways and means of getting the right men into the right places. It is this necessity which at different times has been the justification of different forms of government : monarchy, aristocracy, and democracy are each in turn to be justified according to the circumstances of their age and their constancy to this ideal. In our day each of these has a common enemy— capitalism ; which, as Mr. Chesterton has said, " stands out in history in many curious ways. For the most curious fact about it is that no man has loved it ; and no man has died for it," and yet to-day most men serve it, because it is rare in our society to find a man fulfilling his proper function. The source of this corruption is the growth of the wage system, which, treating labour as a commodity to be bought and sold in the market, denies to men the right and opportunity to use their talents in the way that Nature ordained.

VII

THE EVIL OF LARGE ORGANIZA-
TIONS

IN the last chapter I insisted that the evils which we associate with the wage system to-day are not to be found in the institution of wages as such, but in the dehumanization of the wage relationship which had followed the growth of large organizations, the division of labour, and the misapplication of machinery. I propose now to show that the assumption of Collectivists that large capitalist organizations are more efficient than smaller ones, that they have come to stay, and that they may one day pass into the hands of the workers,[1] are generalizations entirely without foundation in fact, and could only have been conceived by men destitute alike of practical industrial experience and a metaphysical position, defects which, as I have previously pointed out, are characteristic of the Fabian essayists.

Of course, I am quite ready to admit there are certain kinds of modern industrial activities which must in the nature of things be organized on a large scale. It is evident, for instance, that mining, railways, and engineering do not

[1] See Preface, p. 9.

5

admit of small-scale organization ; and in so far as these are to exist in the society of the future, large-scale organization becomes inevitable. Such an admission, however, does not invalidate my general position, which is, that in so far as the element of choice enters, the small organization is to be preferred to the larger one, and that small units must be the basis of industrial reorganization : just as the admission that certain work is perhaps inevitably disagreeable does not invalidate the proposition that it is desirable to make work as pleasurable as possible.

With this truth—that the smaller organization is always to be preferred—firmly planted in our minds, we shall be able to minimize the evils which are inherent in large-scale organization by insisting that every large organization should consist of a multitude of smaller ones which co-operate together. It is evident, moreover, that industry which must be organized on a large scale bulks very much larger to-day than would be the case in a properly ordered society, and it may be that in proportion as society attains to its ideal, large organizations will tend to disappear.

It is to be observed that when the Fabian recommends large organizations as the ideal upon which industry should be modelled in the future, he does not analyse the structure of industry nor deduce the principles of organization from it ; and this for a very simple reason, he is incapable of such analysis. The Fabian Society, as I have said before, is mainly a legal, literary, and medical society, with very few members who have had any industrial experience. The consequence is, that as they do not understand the structure of industry they have become the apologists of the large organization, imagining in their childish ignorance that what is for the moment financially successful is necessarily the best. What the Fabian does is to make use of sophistry and bluff. He tells us that large industries are destined to supplant small ones, because they are more "efficient." Now efficient is an adjective to which no definite meaning can be attached. The French have an excellent word to describe reasoning of this kind. They call it *flou*. Mr. Belloc has translated it for us as wobble-stuff, and when the Fabian talks about large organizations being more efficient than smaller ones he makes use of wobble-stuff, since before it is possible to say whether anything is efficient or not it is necessary to know the purpose or end which it is to serve. On this issue the Fabian has nothing to say. He leaves us entirely in the dark as to the ends for which large organizations are efficient. It is necessary, therefore, that I should explain them. Large organizations are not more efficient for the making of things either useful or beautiful, but they are more efficient for the purpose of making profits, because it is easier for them to make a corner in the market and to speed up the workers, and the simplest proof I can bring in support of this contention is the historical argument that the growth of large organizations in industry has coincided with the substitution of production for use by production for profit. That fact is not only undeniable, but it is equally undeniable that it is the desire for profits which is the reason for their continued growth to-day.

But I shall be told that the large organization is an established fact, and that though it be true that production for profit is the animating principle to-day, production for use will be substituted for production for profit when these organizations pass into the hands of the people. This, again, is a piece of Fabian bluff. It is a pure assumption. The wish is father to the thought. No reasons have ever been given in support of such a contention. And nowadays, when the theory of the nationalization of industry has broken down, it is less plausible than it was, since so long as large organizations obtain, it is difficult to see how industry can ever pass into the hands of the workers, for the simple reason that, apart from the capitalist's activities, industry to-day has no organic structure. When the capitalist affirms that it is his enterprise that keeps things going, I regret to say he is telling the truth. Herein lies the condemnation of the large industry. So rotten have things become, that industry to-day has no life springing from its own roots, but has come to depend entirely upon an external and artificial stimulus to galvanize it into activity from above. Remove this artificial stimulus, due to the desire for profits, and stagnation would speedily result ; for the greater part of our industrial activities have no validity apart from 'the desire for profits. Exclude the motive of profit from such activities, and they would cease to exist.

The large industry necessarily produces for profit because it involves the control of industry by the financier ; and there is no test of a financier's skill except his capacity to produce profits. With the craftsman it is different. He has a natural pride and interest in what he produces, which is possible to a man who actually makes things with his own hands, but which is impossible for a man who can only juggle with figures. Such interest is only possible for the craftsman if he is in business as a small master or is under the direct control of a master craftsman who sympathizes with his aims. This involves small-scale production in small workshops, because it is impossible for a man to manage a large organization and at the same time to work with his hands. The organization of industry on a large scale involves class division,[1] and this

---

[1] In order to avoid confusion, it is necessary for me to explain that I am not condemning the class divisions which a guild hierarchy implies, but such divisions as involve the existence of a class of men without craft traditions who specialize in finance, for the existence of such a class will always be a peril to society. This peril consists in the domination of society by men who think primarily in terms of figures rather than of things ; of prices instead of values ; of quantities rather than qualities. The Collectivist idea of nationalizing industry does not abolish this evil ; it whitewashes it.

is the forerunner of trouble. The financial men are incapable of understanding the needs of craftsmanship. They come to look upon themselves as superior beings because they do not soil their hands and can dress smartly. This is the secret of those feelings of class antagonism which exist in industry to-day, and it is out of these feelings of class antagonism that there arises the determination of the controlling class to drive the men in their employ. Hence speeding-up and production for profit. These things are inseparable from one another. The sooner Socialists recognize the interdependence of large organizations, speeding-up, and production for profit, the sooner we shall find salvation.

Great as are the evils of large organizations already enumerated, there is yet a greater than all these. It is this : they tend to destroy liberty, and their growth is a peril to personal independence. The liberty of a people depends ultimately upon the liberty of the individual, and the liberty of the individual depends in the last resort upon his ability to set up in business on his own account. I am assured that it is because this possibility is becoming daily more difficult of realization that the spirit of liberty is declining in modern society. The reformer who lives in constant fear of losing his job if he attacks capitalism will, in most cases, only be half hearted in his attack. A man's effectiveness as a reformer is relative to his personal independence, and personal independence disappears as the large organization holds sway.

It happens in this way. A man's prospects in life come to depend less and less upon himself—upon his own powers of industry, intelligence, and manliness—and more and more upon his capacity to curry favour with those who are his immediate superiors, whilst against injustice there is no redress. That is why in large organizations the toady is encouraged, and why men of worth and character are apt to be at a disadvantage. When men of character are found in authority they are apt to owe their position to the accidents of the system rather than to the system itself.

It is often said that we are becoming a nation of opportunists, and apart from the working class, this is largely true. The cause is the growth of large organizations. It matters little whether their ownership be vested in a private capitalist company, in the State, or even in a co-operative society. So long as an organization is large, a man's future will depend entirely on the favour of a single individual who, unless he be a man of insight, will inevitably fall into the hands of men who, to secure promotion, play up to him and bully their subordinates.

There is but one remedy for this state of affairs —to get the small holder back into industry, as we are seeking to get him back on to the land, and to limit the use of machinery in a way which makes this possible. We are not justified in looking upon large organizations as we know them to-day as being in any sense of the word permanent institutions. Most of them are rickety, as is natural when we understand the vices inherent in them, for such vices bring about a steady demoralization and make them increasingly costly to run.[1] I believe the growth of speeding-up is in no small degree attributable to the wastage which goes on in these organizations and the necessity of keeping pace with it. Yet large organizations will never yield to a frontal attack until we undermine their intellectual and moral sanction. So long as we worship success, bigness, and cheapness as ends in themselves, we shall continue to be enslaved by them, while in so far as they owe their existence to the possession of natural monopolies and legal privileges there can be no remedy but revolution.

Finally, I would observe that if ever we are to emancipate ourselves from the tyranny of large organizations we shall have to be very clear in regard to our principles. Evil would never come into existence if it did not confer some immediate benefit. It is necessary to resist such temptations ; and the only terms on which it is finally possible to resist them is to be in possession of fixed principles. A study of the degeneration of organizations reveals the fact that every change,

[1] Mr. Raymond Radclyffe, the City Editor of the *New Witness*, in reviewing the share market of the past year (1916) says : " I cannot help thinking that the big shop has seen its best days. There was a time when these enterprises were the best investments possible, but nearly all of them have grown too big, and the management expenses are eating them up " (*New Witness*, January 4, 1917).

which has led eventually to stagnation and decay, has been justified on the grounds of expediency. There is invariably some immediate financial advantage in centralization. This is tangible and definite, and so-called practical men can always point to it. The loss is spiritual, and is not so easily proved, but it can be felt by all men of imagination at the time it occurs. Only at a later date, when the material results are manifested, does this loss become apparent to the many. But it is then too late.

VIII

THE DIVISION OF LABOUR

THE underlying cause of the incompatibility of large organizations with human liberty and happiness is to be found in the system of the division of labour which lies at their base and upon which they are built. In this chapter I propose to examine this system.

Now it goes without saying that in any civilized community labour to some extent must be divided. It is obvious that a man cannot supply all his own needs. To some extent he is inevitably dependent upon others. No sooner did civilization begin to develop than this necessity brought about the specialization of men into different trades. One man became a weaver, another a carpenter, and so forth. In this sense the division of labour may be said to have existed since the earliest times. What, however, in economic language we understand by the system of the division of labour are measures undertaken to increase the output and reduce the cost of production of certain articles of general use by subdividing a trade into a great number of separate branches. This system came into existence during the early part of the

eighteenth century, the classical example being
that eulogized by Adam Smith in *The Wealth
of Nations*, namely pin making, in which industry
it takes twenty men to make a pin, each man
being specialized for a lifetime on a single process.

Now it is apparent that the value which we
place upon such a system as this must depend,
as does our opinion of everything else in this
universe, upon our point of view. Whether we
believe this system to be a blessing or a curse
depends ultimately upon what we conceive to be
the object of industry. If the object of industry
is to cheapen wares as much as possible, then
the system of the division of labour is a real
blessing ; but if, on the other hand, its object is
to produce men and human happiness, then it
must be pronounced the greatest curse that
has ever befallen mankind. The Fabian, reasoning upon fact, and leaving human nature out of
account, regards it as a blessing because it produces goods in a great quantity and cheaply.
I, on the other hand—and I think most workers
will agree with me—believe that it is an unmiti-
gated curse, and that the cheapness which it makes
possible is no compensation for the degradation
of the lives of the producers, which is its inevitable accompaniment. It begins by cheapening
goods ; it ends by cheapening men.

Now, lest any of my readers should imagine
that this system is necessary if the mass of the
workers are to enjoy the comforts of life, I would
point out that without it there would be plenty

for all and to spare if all did their share of the work to be done in the world. In the Middle Ages there was an eight-hours day, and there were sixty saints' days on which the people had holiday, and yet they had sufficient leisure to build our cathedrals and to decorate the most utilitarian objects. Sir Thomas More in his *Utopia*, which was written in the sixteenth century, estimated that if all did their share of work a six-hours day would suffice to do all which needed doing ; and this estimate, I imagine, would take for granted a certain amount of elaborate craft work which, strictly speaking, is a luxury, for to the Mediævalist mind beauty was a necessity. It would appear therefore from this that if the aim of social reform is to reduce the hours of labour as much as possible, then if industry were strictly utilitarian, it would be possible to do what is required by hand labour and without the division of labour in a four- or five-hours day.

I said that the cheapness which results from the division of labour is no compensation for the degradation of the lives of the producers. It is impossible for a man to be happy who is compelled to spend his whole working life in the repetition of a single mechanical operation. If it be true, as Aristotle asserts, that happiness is the result of complete activity or its complement (according to the Hindus) of complete inactivity, then the division of labour must be at the root of endless misery. For what can be worse for a man than to spend his whole life in a narrow and artificial activity, which precludes alike the possibility of spontaneity and rest? For both activity and inactivity must be voluntary if they are to lead to happiness.

We often hear it said nowadays that there is a slump in happiness ; and for the majority I think it is true. It is the effect of this system on our lives. Commencing with such simple things as pins and needles, the principle has been applied first to this and then to that, until in one way or another nearly all of us are enslaved, and everywhere we find that men tend to become increasingly specialized along the lines of one single groove. The corruption has reached the professions, which is the beginning of the end, for when specialization is complete the co-ordinating mind, which is essential to join the specialists together, will no longer be available.

Again, specialization not only leads to confused thinking, for no man can think clearly whose experience of life is confined to a narrow area, but it puts too great a strain upon one aspect of a man's nature. A man can only be really happy when every side of his nature is given opportunity for expression. To force him into a groove is, so far as his soul is concerned, to put him into prison.

The Fabian Essays lead off with the significant dogma that " All economic analysis begins with the cultivation of the earth." This may perhaps be true within certain limits. With equal truth it may be affirmed that " all social analysis begins with the nature of man," and for the purposes of social reconstruction it is the real starting-point, because, as it is necessary to act through men if we are going to change things, a theory of social reconstruction which makes the nature of man the starting-point in its analysis will have a very direct bearing upon human possibilities.

It will not be necessary for me to answer the question : What is man, and what are his possibilities? It will be sufficient for our immediate purpose to affirm that it is natural for man to take pleasure in his work ; and if he is unable to take it, then there is something radically wrong with the conditions of his labour. His instincts will be thwarted and his life will be corrupted at its roots. He will cease to be a normal man, and a feeling of restlessness will overcome him, which feeling, in its reaction upon society, will vitiate all healthy human relation-ships. Thus, hating work, he will desire to accumulate money that he may be relieved of its necessity, whilst he will be unable to find delight in the normal pleasures of life. He will crave excitement. I am assured that the spirit of gambling and speculation, which is such a peril to modern society, has its roots in the monotonous nature of the work to which most men have been condemned by the division of labour and its social implications. False social standards are exalted, and in a thousand and one ways evil influences are set in motion. In a word, " everything is turned upside down," which common phrase is the most perfect definition of the social problem ever enunciated. Things are upside down ; that is the matter with modern society.

Now, it is to be observed that though the system of the division of labour cheapens production, it does not allow the workers to take advantage of the resulting cheapness. The skill of the craftsman is an asset like property. It gives him an effective bargaining power in the market, and so enables him to get a decent wage. But the system of the division of labour demands little or no skill of the individual worker, and the capitalist finds it easy to exploit the unskilled worker. Deprived of his skill, the worker can offer no effective resistance to the tyranny of the capitalist, who can bring in the competition of boy and woman labour to drag down his wages to mere subsistence level. And there can be no remedy so long as this diabolical system is allowed to endure. Fabianism supports it, as it does every instrument of oppression. Speeding-up is nothing new in industry. It is merely the application to skilled trades of a tyranny under which the unskilled have suffered for nearly two hundred years.

I will conclude this chapter with a quotation from Ruskin, in which he directed public attention to this evil sixty years ago. The world would have been much happier would it only have listened to him. It is from *The Stones of Venice*.

We have much studied and much perfected of late the
great civilized invention of the division of labour ; only we
give it a false name. It is not, truly speaking, the labour that
is divided, but the men—divided into mere segments of men
—broken into small fragments and crumbs of life ; so that all
the little piece of intelligence that is left in a man is not
enough to make a pin or a nail, but exhausts itself in making
the point of a pin or the head of a nail. Now, it is a good and
desirable thing, truly, to make many pins a day ; but if we
could only see with what crystal sand their points were
polished—sand of human soul, much to be magnified before
it can be discerned for what it is—we should think that there
might be some loss in it also. And the great cry that rises
from all our manufacturing cities, louder than their furnace
blast, is all in very deed for this—that we manufacture everything there except men ; we blanch cotton, and strengthen
steel, and refine sugar, and shape pottery ; but to brighten, to
strengthen, to refine, or to form a single living spirit never
enters into our estimate of advantages. And all the evil to
which that cry is urging our myriads can be met only in one
way : not by teaching nor preaching, for to teach them is but
to show them their misery, and to preach to them, if we do
nothing more than preach, is to mock at it. It can be met
only by a right understanding on the part of all classes, of
what kinds of labour are good for men, raising them, and
making them happy ; by a determined sacrifice of such
convenience, or beauty, or cheapness as is to be got only by
the degradation of the workman, and by equally determined
demand for the products and results of healthy and ennobling
labour.

There is one comment it is necessary for me
to make on this eloquent passage, and it lies
at the root of Ruskin's failure. He disdained
to preach to the people, not understanding that
reform from above can only be successful on
the assumption that it is met by an impulse from

below. We know better than this to-day. This nightmare out of Bedlam will never come to an end until the people rebel against it and claim their right to be treated as responsible and human beings. So long as they are content to work as the mere cogs in a machine, neither economic nor spiritual emancipation is possible.

IX

MACHINERY AND INDUSTRY

CLOSELY allied with the problems connected with the system of the division of labour is that of machine production. If we decide that the division of labour is a curse, and is the cause alike of the modern unhappiness and the economic servitude of the workers, then it follows that in so far as the use of machinery necessitates this subdivision of function, it can only have evil results. If, also, it be true that the happiness and independence of the workers is the only basis upon which a reasonable and stable society can be built, the use of machinery will need to be limited in such a way as to make this possible.

Socialists are very fond of using the phrase—" Machinery must be the slave of man, and not his master." I wonder how many of those who have expressed their opinions in this way understand the implications of their words, for they are accustomed to suppose that machinery would, of necessity, become the slave of man if its profits or its products were divided among the workers. But is this so? Granted, for the purposes of argument, that the control of machinery might pass into the hands of the workers organized in Guilds, it would be possible for the workers to share its profits or products and to suppress adulteration and jerry work ; but that would not make machinery the slave of man. I am persuaded that there is more in the problem than that—that, indeed, machinery might be owned by the Guilds and its more flagrant abuses abolished, and yet might be the master instead of the slave of man. I contend that the man who spends his whole life in repeating some simple mechanical process is the slave of machinery, though he should be a millionaire.

Such a man might be well-clothed, housed, and fed, and yet the machine would be using him, and not he the machine. If we think more about this matter we shall see that whether machinery is the slave of man or his master is not primarily a question of ownership, but is relative to the size of the machine. In the same way, when we say that " fire is a good servant, but a bad master," we are thinking of its size. A fire that we can control is one whose boundaries are clearly defined—one that we can isolate. The same truth holds good with respect to the control of machinery. *To control it we must be in a position to isolate it.* And this problem, so far as production is concerned, resolves itself finally into a question of size. We can isolate a small machine because we can turn it off or on at will, as is the case with the sewing machine. Such a machine can be used to reduce the amount of drudgery that requires to be done, and enable us to pursue more interesting work. But when machinery is used on a large scale it is different. Those who make use of it must keep it in commission. It must be fed ; and to feed it a man must sacrifice himself mentally and morally to-day. Hence it happens that among all those who are connected with machine production there is an absolute indifference to the interests of everything except the one all-absorbing interest and aim of keeping it going.[1]   That is why the tendency of machine production is to place the control of industry entirely into the hands of a hard and narrow type of man—the financial men, who are undoubtedly the least imaginative section of the community, or, to be more correct, are imaginative only on the lower and selfish plane of thought.

The control of industry by men of this type is inevitable with the extensive use of machinery, because only men of such temperament aspire to its control under these conditions. Modern society finds itself at the mercy of such men because men with broader and more humane sympathies naturally shrink from the narrow and sordid life which the control of machinery and the administration of finance involves. It is to be observed that though Fabians and such-like

[1] There are certain kinds of large machines against which this objection could not always be urged, as, for instance, machinery for pumping or lifting. Against the use of such machinery there can be no objection.

people profess to believe in a glorious future for machinery, they nevertheless prefer to follow occupations not directly connected with it. And so does everybody else who is able to choose, because machine tending is so monotonous and deadening. The only interesting work connected with it lies with the inventor, and with such hand work as still requires to be done. Machine tending is a different matter. It means putting oneself for life into a narrow groove, and every man with imagination seeks to escape from such a fate, as from death. There was some wisdom in that old regulation of the Laws of Manu which forbade the use of all but small machines, it being held that the use of large ones was inimical to society as tending to foster the growth of the commercial spirit. The Laws of Manu, I might add, are the code of laws which underlie the Hindu caste system.

Considerations of this kind suggest the desirability of looking at the problem from all points of view. The final question which we must always ask in considering such issues is not how much more cheaply can goods be produced by extending the use of machinery, but how are such innovations likely to affect the character of men, and how do they affect the position of the young? We shall never be able to secure a more equitable distribution of wealth in the community so long as we lend our approval to methods of production which assist the advancement in society of its most selfish men. Some day, perhaps, we may come to understand that production and distribution are not two separate problems, as economists hitherto have been accustomed to suppose, but are indissolubly linked together in the nature and character of men, and that our failure to solve the problem of distribution is largely to be accounted for by our prejudices regarding methods of production.

I said that in considering this problem we must have regard to the position of the young. In every craft there is much work which, from the standpoint of the skilled craftsman, may be ranked as drudgery, and yet it may not be advisable to do it by machinery, as such work is often very valuable for the purpose of training apprentices. Nowadays, when machinery has absorbed most of this work, the apprentices cannot get proper training. We attempt to remedy this defect by the provision of Technical Schools. We spend a great deal of money on them, and yet we only deal with a small minority of the boys. There is no chance of the principle being given a wider application, not only because of its great cost, but because the growth of machinery has so undermined the demand for skilled labour that there would be no market for these boys if a greater number were trained. Most of this money is sheer waste, and more than counterbalances what is saved by using machinery, while the training which these schools afford is at the best nothing like so good as that provided by the old apprenticeship system. The training has a tendency to become unrelated to practical work. There is something in the atmosphere of a workshop, with its patriarchal spirit, which allows the apprentice to learn a trade in what we may call an organic way. Dr. Coomaraswamy tells us that it is still thought in India that the master's secret may best be learnt by the apprentice in devoted personal service. Needless to say, such relationships are impossible in a technical school. The whole system is too impersonal. Boys who are taught in them are apt to be deficient in the power of adaptability. The reason for this is, as a technical school teacher once explained to me, that as in a workshop there are several men to one boy, the boy gradually becomes a part of a continuous tradition ; whereas, in a technical school, there are many boys to one man, and this sense of tradition is lost. The proper attitude towards technical schools is to regard them at the best as a stopgap. They can never become a substitute for apprenticeship.

Modern industry makes no provision for the young. Large-scale machine production, by creating impersonal relationships, has destroyed our sense of responsibility. Commercialism does not look upon the rising generation as something for which we are responsible, but as material for exploitation. It is impossible to separate the problem of boy labour from those of the division of labour and unregulated machine production. It is only the intellectual cowardice of Collectivists, who felt that to connect them struck at the very

centre of their theory of social evolution, that has
hitherto prevented its recognition. The remedy
presented by Mr. and Mrs. Webb in the Minority
Report of the Poor Law Commission is the last
word in timidity and futility. Instead of finding
the root of the problem in unregulated machine
production, they proposed to give everybody a
technical training. What is to be the nature of
this training I am entirely at a loss to make out,
for they admit the skilled trades are overcrowded,
and that in the unskilled trades are to be found
many who once followed skilled occupations and
have lost their footing owing to the spread of
machinery. So that, finally, it comes to this—
that Mr. and Mrs. Webb hope to solve the problem
of boy labour by teaching boys trades for skill
in which they admit there is no demand. This
is typical of the contradictions in which Collectivists have in these days become involved, and
the fundamental cause of it all is that they have
never dared to face this question of machinery.
If the reform movement is going to follow such
leadership as this, then clearly our social and industrial system can have only one ending. There
will some day be no competence left to run it.

X

MACHINERY AND SOCIETY

In the last chapter I stated the principles which I am persuaded should govern the application of machinery to production. In this one I propose to explain the nature of the evils which have followed the neglect or disregard of them.

Foremost amongst these is the growth of economic instability in our society, which is directly attributable to the misapplication of machinery. A nation to be stable must be so at its base. The workers must neither be insecure nor suffer from a sense of insecurity. They should be able to take their work in a leisurely fashion, and regard themselves as having a job for life ; or, in other words, they must be rooted. If they go from one job to another it should be from choice, and not out of necessity. This, I contend, is the only basis of a stable society ; and if such conditions do not obtain, and uncertainty comes to prevail in people's lives, then it will tend gradually to undermine all the cardinal virtues upon which national stability finally rests. The workers will lose their courage and independence, and will become demoralized, having, indeed, no higher aim than that of keeping going from day to day.

Now, extensive machine production denies security to those engaged in it. It places them at the mercy of forces over which they have no control, nor, I am persuaded, ever can have. The workers are to-day dependent on a new invention, a prospector's luck, a change of tariffs in some foreign land, a change of fashion, and a thousand and one other things ; and though some of these things do not immediately arise from the employment of machinery, but have existed from the earliest times, their evil has become enormously intensified since its introduction. Extensive machine production means quantitative production, and if goods are produced in such quantities that they cannot be consumed for the most part locally, then the element of uncertainty begins to increase. Within certain limits uncertainty is, of course, inevitable. But there is a fundamental difference between the uncertainty which, in an agricultural community, is due to a bad harvest, and the artificial uncertainty caused by overproduction, a change of fashion, or a new invention. The former is inevitable, and as a rule is only temporary ; the latter is purely artificial, and is apt to be much more serious. In America, where industry is more developed, and machinery more misapplied, the changes are often violent. A factory works at full pressure for several months, and then it closes down until it can dispose of its surplus stock. Meanwhile the workers are left to starve. This tendency is inevitable, and will continue to increase so long as we worship machinery in the utterly irrational way we do to-day. To use machinery as a slave is impossible for a people who treat it as a divinity.

Evidence is not wanting that unregulated machine production is carrying us along this path of destruction. Mr. Chesterton once said that modern society was getting top-heavy, and the danger was that it would turn turtle. The Census of Production appears to support this contention, for, according to an article which recently appeared in the *New Statesman*, by Sir Leo Chiozza Money,[1] whose authority on this matter I am prepared to accept, " a surprisingly small proportion of men, women, and children, engaged in occupations for gain, are actual and direct producers of material commodities, whether minerals, agricultural products, or manufactured articles," while there is a " monstrous disproportion of distributors, traffickers, and hangers-on of various kinds, whose work is of little or no economic value, and who serve to attenuate the thin stream of commodities —many of them consisting of rubbish—deliberately and knowingly produced as rubbish—which flows from the places where the real work of the nation is done." Sir Leo does not give us the exact proportions which the useful and useless labour bear to each other ; nor is it necessary. It is sufficient that we know that there exists this

---

[1] "Delimitation and Transmutation of Industries," by Sir Leo Chiozza Money, M.P. (*New Statesman*, March 14, 1914).

monstrous disproportion. Any one with eyes to
see knows this to be true, quite apart from the
corroborative testimony of the Census of Production. Sir Leo offers no explanation of its cause.
He merely states it as a fact, the inference being
that it is to be ascribed entirely to the unequal
distribution of wealth.

Needless to say, to a certain extent this is true ;
but it is not the whole of the truth by any means,
for it is demonstrable that in a far higher degree
the disproportion of useless to useful labour is
due to our excessive use of machinery. Every
time a machine is invented to do useful and
necessary work, which hitherto was done by hand,
it transfers a certain number of men from useful
to useless occupations. It increases the number
of distributors, traffickers, and hangers-on of
various kinds, or, in other words, it turns the
craftsman into a commercial traveller [1] or a maker
of useless commodities. This process will continue until we make up our minds to limit the
use of machinery. It is no use arguing, as Sir
Leo does, that it would be possible, with a strong
central authority, to remedy this defect by re-
distributing the work of the community in such
a way as to transfer men back from useless
to useful work, because it so happens that, as
industry becomes more complex, the establishment of a strong central authority becomes increas-

[1] According to *Advertising and Progress,* by E. S. Hole and
John Hart, the capital invested in distribution to-day is about
three times as great as that invested in actual production,

ingly difficult. Even if one could be established
we should be no better off, for the number of
adjustments required would be legion, and there
is no man living—nor is there ever likely to be
one—who will have sufficient knowledge and experience to get a grip of the endless details
necessary to effect such a delimitation and transmutation of occupations. If there were one, too,
he would be powerless, because he would be confronted with the problem of vested interests. The
truth is, this is not the way things are done.
There is a limit to the successful application of
the principle of control from without, and that
limit has long since been reached. The only
way to grapple with this problem is by giving
application to the principle of control from within,
such as would follow the restoration of the Guilds.

Sir Leo Chiozza Money is a believer in the
extended use of machinery, but he does not believe
in Guilds. He is consistent in his point of view,
for it is almost a certainty that if the Guilds were
restored efforts would be made to regulate
machinery. That is, indeed, one of the reasons
why we want to see them restored. Sir Leo sees
a danger in this, for he says that : " We have to
beware lest we stereotype forms and institutions
which frustrate the proper use of great ideas,"
as the groups or Guilds " would seek to perpetuate
their functions, whether they were useful or not."
If this were true it would be a valid objection,
but I am assured there is no such danger possible.
I deny the possibility of superimposing Guild

organization over latter-day parasitic and useless occupations. Guild organization could only be applied to industries which had a basis in real human needs, and commencing with these, the surplus labour which nowadays is compelled to follow useless occupations would be absorbed as it became possible to regulate machinery. It is strange that Sir Leo should object to Guild organization for these reasons, for it was the realization of the danger of stereotyping men which first opened my eyes to the evils of Collectivism, and led me to place my hopes for the future in the restoration of the Guilds. This stereotyping is now more than a danger ; it is an established fact.

Finally, I would suggest the wisdom of not accepting scientists at their own valuation. We have fallen into a fatal habit of assuming that a thing which is new is in some mysterious way beneficial to society. A new device has only to call itself scientific and it is assumed, without further question, that it is superior in every way to the thing which it seeks to supplant. Such, however, is rarely the case. What scientific men invariably do is to seek the remedy for one evil by creating another, and, generally speaking, a worse. Our memories are very short, or we would be very sceptical about the predictions of scientific men. Their promises are rarely fulfilled, and most of them show no signs of ever being fulfilled. They prophesied that the application of machinery to industry would give the people leisure by reducing the amount of drudgery to be done in the world. Are there any signs of it? Has not precisely the opposite state of things come about? They told us that money-making would make the many rich. Are there any signs of it? Has not again precisely the opposite come about, and have not the masses been precipitated into the most abject poverty the world has ever seen? They told us that Free Trade and universal markets would inaugurate an era of peace and good will amongst nations! Again, I say, are there any signs of it, and are we not exhausting our resources to-day in a competition for armaments? Why should we listen seriously to a point of view with such a record of failure behind it, or to men who make promises which they have no idea how to fulfil ; whose only remedy, indeed, for every evil is to take measures to increase it.

XI

THE ULTIMATE BASE OF INDUS-TRIALISM

THE final answer to Socialists, who imagine that it is possible to remedy the evils of poverty by compromising with Industrialism, is that, if they could be successful in their efforts, Industrialism itself would immediately collapse, for no one could be found to do the objectionable and dangerous work which lies at its base.

Socialists who talk glibly about the blessings of Industrialism are invariably members of the middle class, who profit at the expense of their fellows. Industrialism has brought them many conveniences, and it has also given them opportunities for travel. They dream of a day when the mass of the workers will enjoy the same opportunities, not realizing it is an utterly impossible dream. It is merely a middle-class illusion, for these conveniences are only made possible by the existence in our society of a class of workers who are not so fortunately placed.

In a new country like South Africa it has only hitherto been possible to get such work done by tempting the cupidity of workers who were anxious to make a pile in a short space of time and to return home. In this country the capitalist finds himself to-day under no such necessity. His policy is to sweat the workers. He aims at the deliberate creation of a class of workers so degraded, and with an outlook in life so hopeless, that they will have little option but to do the horrible and dangerous work which lies at the base of industrialism. This he has been able to do because he found such a slave class ready to his hand, which had come into existence as a result of the appropriation of the land by the few and the economic uncertainties which had followed the growth of quantitative production.

Apart from the use which is made of machinery, the most important difference between the present day processes of manufacture and those that obtained in the past is due to the use of chemicals. Nearly all the newer developments of industry which Mr. H. G. Wells, Sir Leo Chiozza Money, and their friends are so anxious to praise have been made possible by the discoveries of our chemists. And what do we find comes about as a result of these discoveries, but an 'utterly ruthless disregard for the claims of human life, which is unparalleled in history? By comparison, the slavery of the Pagan world appears as a quite humane institution. The slave of the past had no personal liberty, but he was generally properly fed, and in other respects his life was tolerable, except in the darkest periods. He was

7

not submitted to that slow physical torture which is the fate, not only of our chemical workers, but of those in a great many other industries which, strictly speaking, may not be classed as chemical ones.   Workers engaged in the manufacture of alkalis, rubber, Portland cement, white lead, aniline dyes, artificial manures, to mention only a few, come from a degraded class, and are slowly poisoned and done to death in order that our industrial system may continue and production be placed on a scientific basis.

There is nothing new in all this.   Facts of this kind were revealed seventeen years ago by Mr. Robert W. Sherard in *The White Slaves of England*, which, prior to its publication as a book, appeared in serial form in *Pearson's Magazine*. A more scathing indictment of Industrialism has never been written.   Mr. Sherard was a member of the Fabian Society, and it might have been expected that when this society found itself in the possession of such information it would have begun to look upon industrialism and the discoveries of science in a new light—that it would have come to the conclusion, not merely that industrialism sweated the workers, but that its whole aim and purpose was at fault.   Such, unfortunately, was not the case.   The glamour of science blinded them to the truth.   Mr. Sherard's book has formed the subject of lectures and articles all over the world.   But official Fabianism allowed the matter quietly to drop, and nowadays there are few Fabians who realize the existence of these horrors. Those who do, tell us that the remedy is to be found in the shortening of the hours of labour and the introduction of safety regulations, etc., which would render such evils, where they were not actually preventable, comparatively harmless.

To me, however, this proposed solution has never been convincing, and for a long time it puzzled me to account for the Fabian attitude towards this problem. Fabians were not without sympathy for suffering, and it is unthinkable that they should regard physical torture as of less importance than poverty. The conclusion at which I eventually arrived was that this attitude was attributable to their materialistic philosophy. It becomes apparent, therefore, that if our ideal of the future is ultimately translatable into the terms of the present, we shall find ourselves in the end committed to the support of the present system. Mr. and Mrs. Webb's acquiescence in speeding-up as their endorsement of the Servile State is ultimately to be accounted for by the fact that with such a limited vision they can see no alternative. And it is the same, I imagine, with respect to their attitude towards our chemical industries. They accept as inevitable, evils whose existence they deplore, because they lack the requisite imagination to see their way to abolish them.

Looking, then, at our chemical industries and dangerous trades from this point of view, the failure of the leaders of the Fabian Society to handle the problem which they present may be traced to their lack of æsthetic insight. The official Fabians thought such evils inevitable, because the products of such industries were desirable. But a man of taste knows better. He looks at things in a different way, and knows that if the taste of the community could be raised, most of these evils would automatically disappear. I should not like to be so rash as to say they would all do so, for there are certain evils which are not to be eradicated entirely in this way. But, in any case, they would be reduced to more manageable dimensions.

To prove exactly how far such a statement is true, it would be necessary to conduct a very wide inquiry into industrial processes ; but it is certainly true, up to a certain point. So far as my investigations have carried me, I have discovered that innumerable things which the artist abominates give rise to dangerous industries. Take the case of lead poisoning, so well known in the Potteries. It is not inevitable. The leadless glaze made with felspar is not dangerous. Why, then, is it not in general use? The answer is because, as the modern public has a debased taste, it demands a high glaze.

And so again with respect to the manufacture of aniline dyes and the bleaching of fabrics, which are dangerous trades. The artist likes dull glazes, broken colour, and a feeling of texture in materials, but the public to-day, destitute of any æsthetic perception and mechanical in its taste, likes an appearance of smartness. It is this smartness,

or trade finish, which Mr. Bernard Shaw is so
anxious to praise, that has created one of the
main sources of demand for chemicals to-day.
Another reason for their use is the growth of
adulteration. It would not be untrue to say that,
as art and the pride of craftsmanship went out
of industry, chemistry came in. Such are the
benefits which science has brought to mankind.[1]
It looks, indeed, as if there were some truth after
all in the old Eastern proverb that " knowledge
is evil."

It is necessary for me to point out that many
of the evils connected with production are increased by the specialization involved in the great
industry. In the old days of small industries and
small workshops, to which the craftsman hopes
to return, many of these dangerous trades formed
part of other trades, and so the evil was not
felt. But as industry has become more and more
specialized, each separate process has tended to
become a trade in itself, and certain men become
specialized on the dangerous part. The Collectivist
is very fond of saying that in the future everybody

[1] " For long to come, if not for ever, science will be the
remorseless enemy of mankind. I see it destroying all
simplicity and gentleness of life, all beauty of the world; I
see it restoring barbarism under a mask of civilization ; I see
it darkening men's minds and hardening their hearts ; I see it
bringing a time of vast conflicts, which will pale into insignificance 'the thousand wars of old' and, as likely as not,
will whelm all the laborious advances of mankind in blood-
drenched chaos" (*The Private Papers of Henry Ryecroft*,
by George Gissing).

will have to take his share of the dangerous work of the world. But he has no idea how he is going to do it. In these circumstances it is necessary to tell him. It is by restoring the small industry. There is no other way.

XII

THE PLACE OF HANDICRAFT

THE conclusion to be drawn from our analysis of the structure of industry is that it is impossible to superimpose Guild organization upon its existing activities. The desire for profits, the division of labour, and the misapplication of machinery, have introduced such a measure of confusion, and created such a host of parasitic trades, that as it exists to-day, industry is incapable of organization except upon a capitalist basis. So long as it remains as it is, the capitalist will inevitably remain master of the position, because industry to-day has no organic structure apart from his activities. As I pointed out in an earlier chapter, it has no life springing from its own roots, but has come to depend upon an external and artificial stimulus to galvanize it into activity from above.

In these circumstances it will be necessary, before taking measures to restore the Guilds, to bring industry back to a healthy and normal state. We must pursue a policy which will enable us to rid ourselves of the incubus of the parasitic trades by the gradual absorption of the workers into the useful ones. The way to do this, in so far as it is an urban problem, is to effect a general revival of handicraft. Such a revival would restore to industry the base which the misapplication of machinery has destroyed. Upon this base we could build. The immediate economic effect of a revival of handicraft would be to relieve the pressure of competition by giving employment to a greater number of workers. The reaction of this upon the position of the workers would be to bring into their lives a greater element of choice, which would enable them to regulate machinery and to transfer their labour where desirable from useless to useful occupations.

Fortunately for us, the pioneer work of such a revival has already been done. Its foundations have been well and securely laid by the Arts and Crafts Movement, which came into existence thirty years ago as a result of the influence of William Morris. There is no way of finding out the truth like that of doing things, and the Arts and Crafts Movement, by attempting to raise the standard of quality in production, has brought into the light of day economic knowledge for which we have much reason to be grateful. The experience of the movement has made an economic analysis of production for quality possible. Its successes and failures each have their lessons to teach, but from the economic point of view we learn more from the failures.

What is the nature of this failure of the Arts and Crafts Movement? It is that it has not attained its real object of stemming the tide of that industrialism which produces shoddy wares, the cheapness of which is paid for by the lives of their producers and the degradation of their users. Nor has it succeeded in bringing beauty back into the lives and homes of the workers, or in freeing art from its dependence on luxury. That the movement has failed in this high endeavour, and exists to-day to produce articles of luxury for the rich, is not its fault. It is its misfortune. Craftsmanship is impossible without intelligent patronage, and it has been the misguided patronage of the public, who failed to appreciate the significance of the movement, and therefore to support it in the way it desired to be supported, that has diverted its energies into the wrong channels. There was certainly some excuse for the public, for the movement was largely experimental, and it was unfortunately not accompanied by a propagandist movement which would have explained its aims. The consequence is that the public have failed to understand that the kind of work produced has been too often a matter of necessity rather than of deliberate choice.

The layman to-day, having observed that the craftsmen connected with the movement are mostly concerned with the production of works of a decorative and ornate character, and realizing their superiority over machine-made articles, has conceded the case for craftsmanship in this sphere of work. It is rare nowadays to meet

a man of education who would deny it. We may
conclude, therefore, that within the sphere of
æsthetics the battle has been won. But this is
as far as we have gone. The implications of
this admission are not understood by sociologists
generally, who imagine that it is possible for
the more highly skilled crafts to be organized
on a basis of hand production, while the more
roufine kinds are given over to the machine.
This is the issue which has hitherto divided
Socialists and craftsmen. It is fundamental, for
experience has proved to the craftsmen that to
compromise is to be lost.

It is not, then, out of mere pig-headedness
that the craftsman demands that the use of
machinery shall be limited to the extent which
I suggested in an earlier chapter. In practice,
craftsmen are too often compelled to compromise
to-day. But those who are clear-headed know
that they are making terms with the devil for
permission to live ; for it is finally impossible
to have a body of cream without a body of milk
underneath it. If the milk is there, then the
cream will rise to the top ; but if instead of
milk we only get chalk and water, then no cream
will be forthcoming. The highly skilled craftsman knows only too well that in modern industry
he lives by suffrance. He knows that he is part
of an old order which is fast disappearing ; that
the ground is rapidly slipping away from under
his feet, and that unless the tide of machine
production can be stemmed the present genera-

tion of craftsmen will have no successors. It will be impossible to train a small group of highly skilled men to succeed them, because it will be impossible to select them for the purpose of training. The young apprentice is an unknown quantity ; and it is only by providing opportunities for training and work for the many that the great craftsmen become possible. The well-known craftsmen connected with the Arts and Crafts Movement are the few among a great mass of inferior craftsmen who have survived because of their superior gifts and opportunities. Doubtless there are many among our machine workers who might have attained to the same prominence and distinction had they enjoyed similar advantages and opportunities, for it is opportunity that makes the man. The powers within us lie dormant until the chance comes along which quickens them into life. Hence it is, when I hear a man talk about the need of equality of opportunity, I invariably ask his opinion of machine production. His answer to that question tells me finally exactly where he stands, for machinery has been the great destroyer of this equality. It has created the most effective class barrier ever devised. A quotation from Dr. Coomaraswamy's *Mediæval Sinnalese Art* will drive my point home. Speaking of the relationship existing between machinery and industry, he says :—

Not merely is the workman through the division of labour no longer able to make any whole thing, but it is impossible for him to improve his position or to win reward for excellence in the craft itself. Under Guild conditions it was possible and usual for the apprentice to rise through all grades of knowledge and experience to the position of a master crafts-man. But take any such trade as carpet-making by power-loom under modern conditions. The operator has no longer to design or weave in and out the threads with his own fingers or to throw the shuttle with his own hand. He is employed, in reality, not as a weaver, but as the tender of a machine. . . . That craft is for him destroyed as a means of culture, and the community has lost one more man's intelli-gence, for it is obviously futile to attempt to build up by evening classes and free libraries what the day's work is for ever breaking down. It is no longer possible for culture and refinement to come to the craftsman through his work ; they must be won, if won at all, in spite of his work ; he must seek them in a brief hour snatched from rest and sleep, at the expense of life itself. . . . There can be no quality of leisure in his work. In short, machine production absolutely forbids a union of art with labour.

The reason we do not readily recognize this is because we have come to connect the idea of culture with book-learning. But craft culture is a far better base to build upon. The real education comes by doing things. To do a piece of honest work and to try to place it on the market will teach a man ultimately more about sociology than reading a thousand books on the subject, because it gives him a firm grip of the basic facts. The man who never has had this practical experience cannot be quite sure of his fundamentals, and so tends to find himself at the mercy of intellectual fashions. The instability of the modern mind is due ultimately to the separation of the mass of the people from actual work. Machinery, in separating them from it, has destroyed the base of their culture, and intellectual stability will never return until this base is restored. It is interesting in this connection to know that in China, where the people reverence above all things literature and learning, the idea of literature pursued as a separate profession is not favoured. Every literary man is supposed to be more or less of a craftsman—a painter or a musician. And I think the Chinese are right, for literature divorced from its base in actual work is apt to lead to superficiality.

XIII

THE ETHICS OF CONSUMPTION

If there is one thing more than another which the experience of the Arts and Crafts Movement has proved conclusively, it is the impossibility of any group of craftsmen, however gifted —and in this connection it is well to remember that the movement secured the active support of the cleverest architects and artists of its day— to effect any widespread reform, apart from the organized support of the public. Without a propaganda movement to teach the public, the craftsman found himself very much at the mercy of the existing demand. A German poet has said that " against stupidity even the gods fight in vain," and on the æsthetic side of things the British public is peculiarly stupid. It utterly fails, for the most part, to understand the meaning and purpose of art. It fails to realize that beauty and sweetness are essential elements of any human perfection, and that art, when it is vital, enters into every operation of industry, from the making of bricks to the highest flights of the imagination. It conceives of art as a veneer or decoration superimposed upon, or added to something which would otherwise be ugly. The idea that art is organic and inherent in the nature of a thing from the moment of its inception has never so much as entered the public mind. And yet it is precisely the perception of this truth which is the essence of the artist. He recognizes that there is a right way of doing everything, and that right way is art.

The ordinary British philistine will not admit this. Being without the finer æsthetic perceptions, which alone can enable a man to determine which is the right way of doing things, and lacking that spirit of humility which in the ages of great traditions made him conscious of his ignorance, he seeks to evade the problem by affirming that everything is a matter of taste. In one sense this is true, but not in the sense in which he means it. Every great artist has a personal bias. It is this bias that constitutes his individuality, and we are justified in respecting such differences as arise from the individuality of great artists. These, however, are fundamentally different from the differences which arise from the idle fancies of undisciplined tastes, for the great artist submits his taste to a stern discipline. His spontaneity is the flower of that discipline, and it is just in proportion as a man can submit himself to this discipline that he takes his rank as an artist. I cannot insist too strongly upon the need of recognizing this truth. It is fundamental, and it will remain impossible to restore a tradition of art and handicraft until it is realized. The absence of any such tradition or common language of design is at the root of our difficulties to-day, for when every one is, as it were, speaking a different language, artists have little chance of being understood. Now, a tradition bears the same relation to art as the command of language does to speech. Without a language it would be possible for a man to make noises, but words are necessary to enable him to express himself, and he must possess a good vocabulary if he wishes to convey his ideas and to make his meaning clear to others. So in respect to a tradition of art ; without it, it is simply impossible for any man to design or express himself intelligently. The only way to recover such a medium of expression for the use of all is by the exercise of a rigid discipline in matters of taste.

When we realize how utterly false is the popular idea of art to-day, it is not surprising that it is neglected. Truth to tell, in so far as the art of to-day does approximate to the popular notion there is no purpose in supporting it. The sooner it dies a natural death the better. But real art is a different matter. No nation neglects its claims without being made to suffer for it, and this not only in the hideousness and rawness of its external life, but in a decline of general intelligence and in the growth of economic difficulties. For all these things are related to each other in subtle ways, and the great thinkers of every age have recognized it. Could we see

that terrible monster, modern European materialistic civilization in its true light, we should realize
that it owes its existence in no small degree
to our neglect of the arts and their sweetening
and refining influence. The best proof I can
bring of this is that art and our civilization are
antipathetic, not merely in the material, but in
the spiritual sense. It is impossible to produce
beautiful things for people who think like the
moderns do when they are determined to have
their own way. In this respect Socialists as
a body are no better than other people. Indeed,
I often incline to think they are worse ; for
their fatal habit of relating every evil in society
to the growth of the economic problem is apt
to blind them to aspects of truth, the recognition
of which is not only indispensable to the solution
of the problems of art, but of the economic
problem itself.

I said that the popular idea of art was that
it is a veneer or decoration added to something
which would otherwise be ugly. This fallacy
ultimately accounts for the neglect of the Arts
and Crafts, because it leads the public to suppose
that beauty is necessarily expensive. That, of
course, is true, in so far as it depends upon
honest workmanship and the use of good material,
but that is all the truth there is in it. A table
may be in good or bad proportion, it may be
of a pleasing or offensive colour, but neither proportion nor colour has anything particularly to
do with the cost. In each case what makes the

difference is whether the designer has an eye for these things. Many artistic products are cheap, as the peasant arts of all countries which have not been exploited by commercialism bear witness. But the public neglect them. With their fixed idea that art is something added, and therefore costly, they refuse to buy such things. They prefer shoddy made imitations of more expensive forms of design. The consequence is that beautiful things which are inexpensive tend to go off the market. This stupid attitude of mind makes it difficult for the artist to be perfectly straightforward in his dealings with the public. He never knows what to charge. In many cases, if he charges a fair price and the price is low, they refuse to buy, on the assumption that it is not good work. If, knowing this, he prices his work high, as likely as not they will say that they cannot afford it. In a word, the artist in his dealings with the public to-day not infrequently finds himself between the devil and the deep blue sea. The public become the prey of sharks of all kinds, because it is almost impossible for honest men to handle them. They have only themselves to blame. It is this kind of nonsense that defeated the Arts and Crafts movement in its original intention, and it is this kind of nonsense that the capitalist knows how to exploit. It is the secret of half of his power.

There is another reason for the neglect of the Arts and Crafts. It is a spiritual failure. It

is one of the paradoxes of our age that the public
do not appear to mind how much they spend
upon things of a temporary nature, but they
grudge every penny spent upon things of permanent value. The proprietor of a West-End
gallery where works of handicraft are sold, told
me recently that ladies who would not mind giving
fifteen or twenty guineas for a hat which only
lasts a few months and which probably only costs
as many shillings to make, yet will consider
an article of craftsmanship at a similar price,
which represents real value in labour quite apart
from its æsthetic qualities, as outside their reach.
It is perfectly extraordinary, when you get behind
the scenes, to witness the vagaries of the public
or to account for their motives in expenditure.
No matter how huge a person's income may
be nowadays, he rarely thinks he can afford
to buy anything of permanent value. The vast
mass of people fritter away their incomes in
all kinds of senseless extravagance. They know
no limit to personal expenditure, and are mean
and contemptible in every other direction. And
this spirit is not only confined to the rich. It
is spreading to every class of society, down to
the lowest. Have we not heard what the factory
girl spends on dress?

Ruskin spent most of his life in trying to
convince people that political economy is a moral
science. He went to the root of the problem
when he said : " The vital question for individual
and for nation is not, How much do they make?

but, To what purpose do they spend?" It is a fruitful idea, and it receives ample corroborative testimony from the writings of the Chinese philosopher, Ku Hung Ming. He says :—

The financial distress of China and the economic sickness of the world to-day are not due to insufficiency of productive power, to want of manufactures and railways, but to ignoble and wasteful consumption. Ignoble and wasteful consumption in communities, as in nations, means the want of nobility of character in the community or nation to direct the power of industry of the people to noble purposes. When there is nobility of character in a community or nation, people will know how to spend their money for noble purposes. When people know how to spend their money for noble purposes, they will not care for the what, but for the how—not for the bigness, grandeur, or showiness, but for the taste, for the beauty of their life surroundings. When people in a nation or community have sufficient nobility of character to care only for the tastefulness and beauty of their life surroundings, they will want little to satisfy them, and in that way they will not waste the power of industry of the people, such as in building big, ugly houses and making long, useless roads. When the power of industry of the people in a community or nation is nobly directed and not wasted, then the community or nation is truly rich, not in money or possession of big, ugly houses, but rich in the health of the body and the beauty of the soul of its people. . . . Ignoble and wasteful consumption not only wastes the power of industry of the people, but it makes a just distribution of the fruit of that industry difficult.

XIV

THE TYRANNY OF THE MIDDLEMAN

THE idiosyncrasies of the purchasing public, by making it difficult for honest men to deal with them, result in placing power in the hands of sharks of various kinds. It goes without saying that such men do not lose the opportunity thus presented to them of strengthening their hold on the public. By means of a device in all respects analogous to the confidence trick of ill repute, the middleman has rendered his position, for the time being, impregnable.

Now the confidence trick, as is well known, is a dodge for imposing on simple-minded people by securing their confidence in the first instance, and then using it later for the purpose of swindling them. There are, of course, commercial possibilities in the idea, and our large distributing houses have not been backward in discovering them. It has become the chief corner-stone of their monopolies. The *modus operandi* is as follows : The custom and confidence of the public are secured in the first place by tempting their cupidity, and then advantage is taken of the reputation for cheapness thus created to sell them something at an exorbitant price. In the furniture trade, for instance, certain things in general demand, such as chests of drawers, bureaus, chairs, small tables, etc., are not only invariably sweated and jerried, but as often as not are sold without profit, while larger pieces, such as dining-tables, sideboards, bookcases, etc., carry good profits. Again, the simpler kinds of furniture are sold at cost price, and the more elaborate pieces at an exorbitant one. Facts of this kind are well known to everybody, but the social and economic implications of the practice are little understood.

Now, although this system of manipulated prices is to the advantage of large firms, it is not in the interests of the public, who are made to pay, on the whole, more for what they have to buy than would be the case with straightforward dealing. But what is worse than this is that it is utterly fatal to the small man, and defeats the ends of those who are working for industrial reform. The reason is simple. In a state of things in which the selling price of any particular article bears little or no relation to the actual cost of production, it is apparent that it is only possible to make a business pay by dealing in a large variety of goods. The small man cannot do this, and the craftsman finds not only that it limits the range of his activities, but that it destroys public confidence in him.

The craftsman, like all persons of taste, hates the meretricious ornament with which commercial firms spoil their products, and he desires to promote a taste for simple, straightforward design of good proportion. But he finds that if he knocks off five shillingsworth of cheap ornament he knocks five pounds off the selling price of the piece, for the public compares his price with the goods that are sold without profit for the purpose of creating a market for the sham ornamental ones, and this destroys public confidence in him. Even when a person can afford to pay, he imagines the craftsman is asking a fancy price. Machinery, it is true, is the enemy of craftsmanship, but a far greater enemy in the immediate sense is this system of manipulated prices, which checkmates the craftsman absolutely while it secures the market for commercial firms. The paradox about this commercial confidence trick is that it operates to destroy public confidence in honest men.

Exactly to what extent this system obtains it would only be possible to say after long and careful investigation. It certainly does so in all trades in which the element of taste enters, and which are subject to the control of the middleman. This is natural, for such trades lend themselves so perfectly to bluff and humbug when handled for commercial purposes. Generally speaking, the middleman in these trades is an interloper. In a healthy society he would not exist, but the craftsman would work direct for the public, for in the long run it is only possible for him to produce beautiful things if he works in this way. In catering for a definite and known public the craftsman finds himself. But when he is separated from it, as is too often the case to-day, he suffers from an inability to focus his ideas, and his work rapidly degenerates.

A consideration of such issues testifies to the distance we have wandered from the path of righteousness in our economic arrangements. The true function of the middleman is to bring together the producer and consumer for their mutual benefit, and in certain departments of trade he is indispensable. But in trades like the furniture trade he is an intruder, and has usurped functions which do not properly belong to him. The best proof of this is that in such a trade his whole aim and purpose is not to bring the producer and consumer together for their mutual benefit, but to keep them apart for his own.

The growth of the power of the middleman is one of the most alarming symptoms of the age, for it means finally the passing of the control of industry out of the hands of the actual makers and producers of things into the hands of financiers pure and simple, who have no interest in things apart from considerations of profit and loss. This is an unmixed evil, not merely because such men will lack that sense of honour in respect to the tradition of a trade which is the birthright of every craftsman, but because this change lies at the root of the intellectual rot which has over-taken the modern world.

Of course, it is easy to understand why the middleman has become so powerful in modern society. It is one of the results 'of quantitative production. In the old days of qualitative production local markets obtained, and the producer and consumer were in direct relations with each other. The middleman confined his attention to such things as could not be produced locally. But with the introduction of the system of the division of labour and the invention of machinery goods of every kind became too numerous to be disposed of locally. It became necessary to go further and further afield in search of markets, so little by little the middleman grew in importance. Still, for a long time he remained the middleman. He did not aspire to the control of production, which was still regarded as the function of the man with technical training. The change which is increasingly transferring the control of industry into the hands of men without any such training is due to the pressure of competition. So long as demand exceeded supply, the technical man came to his position as the controller of industry as a matter of course. But with the growth of large organizations and the increase of the pressure of competition, a time came when the technical man could no longer set up in business on his own account, for it was necessary to make sure of the market before starting ; and the only man who could do this was the commercial traveller or the man possessed of capital, who was in a position to spend huge sums on advertising. Hence it has come about that the middleman, in his capacity as financier, has succeeded to

the technical man in the control of industry. The
consequence is, not only that technical competence
has ceased to command its proper remuneration,
but that it has ceased to be respected. And
ceasing to be respected, it is suffering a decline.
" Why should I fag to make myself competent,
when nowadays incompetent men succeed best? "
was the reply I got recently from an apprentice
whom I had criticized for his indolence. And
I found it difficult to answer, for what he said
was only too true.

I said the growth of the power of the middleman
is one of the most alarming symptoms of the age.
How to destroy this power is the problem of
industrial reformers. Economists who neglect it
and discourse about the relations of the producer
and the consumer are really living in the eighteenth
century, since neither of them has any real power
to-day. They have both been enslaved by the
middleman in his capacity as financier.

XV

THE STRIKE FOR QUALITY

PASSING on to consider ways and means of emancipating the producer and consumer from their enslavement by the middleman, two possible and complementary lines of action present themselves. One is to attack the problem from the position of the producer, the other is to attack it from that of the consumer. Let us consider it in the first place from the position of the former.

Now, from the point of view of the producer in his capacity of wage-slave, the term middleman may be taken to connote anybody who lives by the exploitation of labour, whether he be merchant, shopkeeper, or actual employer. The employer to-day is a middleman in the sense that he treats labour as a commodity to be bought in the cheapest market. He has succeeded in depressing wages by taking advantage of the economic weakness of the wage-earner, and the workers have failed for the most part to resist his encroachments. The reason for this is, I think, that the workers have hitherto failed to perceive exactly where the weakness of the employers really is to be found.

Instead of choosing their own ground and fighting for the maintenance of a standard in production, where they would be tactically strong, they have allowed the employers to fight them on economic grounds, where they are the weaker. To strike for quality would indeed hit the employers in a very tender place. They would find an attack of such a kind difficult to meet. No firm could afford to have all the little tricks and dodges by which it seeks to cheapen production brought to the public notice. The workers ought to play this card for all it is worth, and they would find themselves in a position not only to get recognition, but higher wages. Moreover, it would secure public sympathy and support for the Unions. They would gain in prestige.

So long as the Unions fight only for higher wages and shorter hours, the public not unnaturally suppose that they have no other interest in life except to get as much for doing as little as possible. But a strike for quality would raise the plane of the struggle. The capitalists for once would be seen in their true colours as rogues and tricksters. They would no longer be able to hide their baseness by making a scapegoat of the British working man. The truth would be out, and capitalism would lose its last moral support.

I feel well advised in recommending this line of action, not only because of the immediate benefits which would accrue from it, but because it is an indispensable step which must be taken before the Guilds can be restored. Let us always remember that a Guild is a privileged body, and privileges are impossible without responsibilities. It is not to be expected that the public could be persuaded to grant privileges to men unless they could be assured that they would not be abused. Sooner or later this issue is bound to be raised. And we shall be in a much better position to face it if we can bring evidence to show that the workers are actively interested in the maintenance of a standard of quality in production. Trade Unionists should take to heart the lesson which the regulation of the Mediæval Guild system teaches us—that the best way to protect the standard of life of the craftsman is ultimately to protect the standard of quality in craftsmanship.

In the affirmation of this truth is to be found the most fundamental divergence from Collectivist opinion. Collectivists always talk as if the social problem was entirely a matter of detailed arrangement. They seem to be quite unconscious of the fact that in society there is a constant struggle between right and wrong, and that that struggle can never be eliminated. It is inherent, and in the very constitution of things. What, however, we may do is to raise the plane of the struggle. When we talk about the need of a redistribution of the wealth of the community, we are apt to forget that the existing struggle for wealth is the result of emptying life of its content, and that it can only be by bringing back into life the things which filled it in the past that the economic motive may be brought again into subjection. The only way of finally combating the evils consequent upon the pursuit of a low motive is by exalting the claims of a higher one. So long as this emptiness is allowed to continue, avarice will remain to fill the vacuum, and I think that so long as the battle is fought primarily according to the dictates of avarice the capitalists will continue to triumph, for with them it is the dominating motive, whereas with the workers it is a regrettable necessity. When I say this, I am not unmindful of the fact that the appeal to the avarice of the many has served a certain immediate purpose in creating that spirit of unrest which is necessary to the solution of the social problem, and that the motive of the Socialist movement has been idealism rather than avarice. Avarice is a powerful weapon for destructive purposes, and in so far as it is necessary to work for the destruction of the present order of society we have perhaps no option but to use it. But we must not forget that it is useless for the purposes of reconstruction. The spirit of co-operation is antipathetic to it. Self-sacrifice rather than self-interest must be its corner-stone.

Looked at from this point of view, the present situation is paradoxical, and its contradictions are, perhaps, only to be reconciled on the basis of the old idea of co-operation within the group and warfare outside of it. Any way, we can be sure that at the present juncture we are right in advocating the strike for quality, for in it both motives will come into play. The higher the workers can raise the standard of production, the easier it will be for them to get control of industry, because the financier is ultimately incapable of organizing industry on a basis of quality. Only the craftsman can do that. The preference of the financier for quantity rather than quality is easily understood. If he produces for quality he is dependent upon the actual workers in a far higher degree than if he produces for quantity. In the former case he must give great attention to detail, and must choose his men carefully with regard to their special aptitudes. But in the latter one man is as good as another. All he wants is unskilled men whom he can sweat and bully, and this more accords with his temperament and intelligence. Hence it is the more the workers can raise the standard of quality in production, the more they will limit the range of the capitalists' activities, and will finally succeed in exorcising him to the nether regions from whence he arose in response to the incantations of our orthodox economists.

The protection of a standard of excellence in craftsmanship was, as I observed in an earlier chapter, the vitalizing principle of the Guilds.

The nearer we approach this ideal, the more we shall see the necessity for a revival of Guilds in their old form. A criticism which has often been hurled at Trade Unions is that by insisting upon equality of payment they offered no inducement to the workman to become expert in his craft. It has generally been made by the opponents of Trade Unionism, and when used to account for the decline of quality in production it is, as an explanation, beneath contempt.

But it contains an element of truth all the same. The Mediæval Guilds had two rates of pay, one for the masters and another for the journeymen of the craft. It is a natural division, and one which I think it will be desirable to revive in the future. Wages must not be allowed to be settled by competition, but it is desirable that excellence be rewarded. Some day, perhaps, such a principle might be reduced to practice. But the Unions will need to secure recognition first.

Finally, I must answer a possible objection to this strike for quality. It will be said that the poor cannot afford wares of a good quality. To this I can only answer that it is not finally true. Our cheap wares to-day are really very costly, because they do not last long. Further, it is necessary to add that the best firms would welcome strikes for quality, as such a policy would protect them against the competition of unscrupulous rivals who undercut their prices and do dishonest work. This competition reacts also against the interests of the working class, for the lowering of the standard of production ends finally in a lowering of the wages and the standard of life of workers, for it places the control of industry in the hands of a less scrupulous class of employer.

XVI

THE ELIMINATION OF THE MIDDLEMAN

THE basis of the workers' revolt against the tyranny of the middleman and financier must be the strike for quality. But strikes at the best are negative measures, and if the middleman is to be eliminated, it can only be by means of action of a positive kind.

The true function of the middleman, as I have already pointed out, is to bring the producer and consumer together for their mutual benefit, and in so far as he fulfils that function he performs a necessary service to society. Unfortunately, to-day he is not content to confine his actions to his legitimate sphere. In invading the crafts he has usurped functions which do not properly belong to him, for craftsmanship is only possible when the public and the craftsman are known to each other. Otherwise the craftsman comes to be dictated to by the salesman, which with men who have an interest in their work is an intolerable tyranny. In these circumstances it will be necessary for us to differentiate between the two types of industry which nowadays are controlled by the middleman, namely those in which he performs a legitimate function and those in which he is an intruder.

In the Middle Ages the distribution of wares was in the hands of the Guild merchants. Yet, though I advocate the revival of the Guilds in the sphere of production, I do not think it is desirable to revive them in the sphere of distribution. We are safe in leaving the production of craftsmanship in private hands when controlled by Guilds, for, as the craftsman comes to have a pride in the work of his hands, he naturally retains a high sense of honour in his trade relationship. But with occupations connected with buying and selling it is different. The temptations of gain are there too strong to be resisted by the average human being, and so it is not desirable to leave them in private hands. In so far, therefore, as the middleman is inevitable, we shall, I think, be well advised to support the Co-operative Movement [1] in its efforts to supplant him, but with this proviso, that it is desirable to place a limit to the size of each separate society, as there is no other way of safeguarding the movement against the vices of bureaucracy.

[1] While we support the Co-operative Movement, let us remember its limitations. "Economic co-operation runs to quantity, because quantity is something that can be proved to everybody's satisfaction; meanwhile, quality, which is incapable of proof, is apt to suffer" (*From the Human End*, by L. P. Jacks).

So far, so good. We may safely look to the Co-operative Movement to eliminate the middleman where hitherto he has been indispensable. But, as I have already pointed out, in certain fields of industry the middleman is an intruder, and we are not justified in allowing even the Co-operative Societies to trespass on the domains of the craftsman, for the problem here is not how to capture the trade of the middleman, but how to dispense with his services altogether. This problem is not to be solved by the ordinary operations of demand and supply. Before it will be possible to bring the craftsman and the public into mutual and reciprocal relationships with each other it will be necessary to restore public confidence in the integrity of the craftsman and to expose the tricks of the middleman by means of an active propaganda movement on the craftsman's behalf. In connection with such a movement there might be established what I might call " introduction agencies," which would aim at bringing the public and craftsmen into direct contact with each other. Such agencies would need to be subsidized in some way if they were to be effective. It would be impossible for an agency which lived by commissions to expose the system of manipulated prices by which the middleman has established his monopoly, for if it did it would not be believed. Moreover, if it lived by commissions it would be compelled to keep the craftsman and the public apart as the middleman does.   This has always been the difficulty connected with galleries which exhibit arts and crafts.   The reason why such galleries have invariably departed from their original purpose is that their financial basis can only be maintained by keeping the craftsmen in the background.

At first an agency of this kind would have to make use of such craftsmen as it found at its hand.   But as its position became more secure and it came to promote the interests of new men, it would be able to facilitate a transition towards a revival of Guilds.   At a later date, when the machinations of the middlemen had been thoroughly exposed, such agencies could be financed by the Guilds until such time as local markets were restored, when they would become unnecessary.

To what extent organization on this basis is possible it is difficult to say ; but production in small workshops is very much more general than is usually supposed.   London and Birmingham are full of small workshops.   An enormous percentage of the goods which are sold in the West End are still made in small workshops, and these workshops are likely to continue, for factory conditions do not lend themselves to the production of goods which require taste and discrimination on the part of the workers.   Some of the goods so produced carry enormous retail profits, and it would be expedient to make a start with them, as by taking away from the middleman the most profitable part of his trade he would be compelled in self-defence to raise his prices for those things which are sold at less than their real value. This raising of prices would enable us to lift certain trades out of the sweated condition in which they find themselves to-day.

XVII

THE DECENTRALIZATION OF INDUSTRY

HITHERTO in my analysis I have treated the social problem as a purely industrial affair, leaving out agriculture. This order was inevitable, because, as we mostly live in towns nowadays, we are accustomed to view things primarily from the industrial standpoint. There is no harm in this so long as we clearly recognize that the industrial problem is in its ultimate analysis inseparable from the agricultural one. I must insist upon this, for though Collectivists view an agricultural revival with a certain sympathy, they nevertheless utterly fail to recognize its fundamental importance. They are inclined to accept the fact that we are an industrial community and to seek a solution of industrial problems as separate and detached issues.

This, however, is impossible. The fact that we have to such a large extent become an industrial community is precisely what makes the social problem so difficult to handle. " A society," says Mr. Lowes Dickinson, ." that is to be politically stable must be economically independent." That opinion receives ample corroboration from the testimony of history. Communities which have been more or less self-contained have persisted for thousands of years, but no community which has once become dependent upon an extensive foreign trade has retained its prosperity for over a limited period. The history of Carthage and Athens, as of Venice and Genoa, demonstrate the fleeting nature of such prosperity. The explanation is simple. The more a nation becomes dependent upon foreign trade, the more it tends to find itself at the mercy of forces which it is powerless to control.

It is impossible to resist the conclusion that so long as industry is dependent upon foreign markets so long will the workers continue to be exploited, because an extensive foreign trade is dependent ultimately upon capitalist adventurers. The workers become parasitic upon the capitalist, because he alone can find the market. It is all very well to talk about abolishing the capitalist, but so long as industry is dependent upon foreign markets he remains indispensable, because only a man whose control of labour is absolute can act with the promptness and decision necessary to adjust the labour of the workers to the uncertainty and fluctuations of distant markets. In other words, so long as industry is dependent upon foreign markets production will be very much of a gamble, and such a condition, I am persuaded, is incompatible with the democratic organization of industry.

Once the fact is grasped that the economic dependence of the workers is bound up with an extensive foreign trade, as it is with large industries and the division of labour, it follows that their emancipation is bound up with small industries and local markets. Only under such conditions have the workers a chance. The master of a small workshop can only maintain his foothold amid stable economic circumstances, such as obtain with local markets. If his market is thousands of miles away he inevitably falls under the control of the financier or middleman. The same thing would happen if the workers were organized into Guilds. They would come to be dependent upon a financial class of men who organized the market for them, and, like capitalists, they would be compelled to resort to the same tricks to hold it. But if agriculture were revived the home market would become available. The workers would have their feet on a solid economic foundation. If they were sure of the home market they could engage in foreign trade to a limited extent, and no harm would come to them, because the home market would guarantee their independence. But to be absolutely dependent upon foreign markets is a different matter. It is to place themselves at the mercy of economic forces which they are powerless to control.

Looking at our industrial system from this point of view, it is evident that the large industry, though perhaps here and there inevitable, will not, to anything like the same extent, bulk so largely in the future as it does to-day. It is evident, for instance, that we shall need fewer railways, their present abnormal development being due to the growth of cross distribution and the aggregation of population into towns. With a more reasonable distribution of population between urban and rural areas, and the revival of small workshops and local markets, which we may safely anticipate in the future, railways will shrink into comparative insignificance. I cannot endorse Mr. H. G. Wells's prediction that we shall travel more and more in the future —though we doubtless will in the immediate future—because this tendency is necessarily accompanied by a growth of social instability which sooner or later must provoke a reaction. After all, the excessive travelling of to-day is largely a reaction against the ugliness of our overgrown towns. But when beauty once more finds a place in our life surroundings, we may expect that the present restlessness will tend to disappear.

It is evident that if ever we are to realize such a state of society as I have sketched, trade relationships will need to be very carefully regulated. We shall not be able to leave ourselves at the mercy of the whimsicalities of Free Trade, for economic stability is impossible in a community which places the workers at the mercy of fluctuations of prices or subjects them to the danger of the importation of sweated goods from other lands. On the contrary, while we approve of the principle of Protection—for the principle of Protection is identical with that of privilege which underlies the Guild System—and must give it our support, we must see to it that it is administered in the interests of society as a whole, and not merely in the interests of such capitalists as find themselves in a position to bring pressure to bear upon the Government to secure privileges for themselves. Our policy must be the protection of the standard of life of the workers and of quality in craftsmanship, which, as I have before explained, go together. But this involves a revival of the Mediæval principles of fixed prices. Protection without fixed prices and without Guild control opens wide the gate of corruption. There are political possibilities, I think, in this idea. The workers might secure privileges for themselves by supporting Protectionists. But they would need to be very careful to see that they came out right. It is not practical politics to-day, but it might be to-morrow.

Lest any of my readers should imagine a system of fixed prices is impracticable, I might say that building contracts to-day are largely based on such a system. In a builder's estimate most of the prices will be taken direct from Laxton's *Builders' Price Book*. The variations are confined to a few items, where the builder exercises his own judgment. In Lancashire also the cotton operatives have a most elaborate system of piece-work rates, which are arranged between the Trade Unions and the employers.

XVIII

THE REDISTRIBUTION OF POPULATION

A FRANK recognition of the fleeting nature of the national prosperity which is based upon an extensive foreign trade would carry us a long way towards the formulation of a true social policy. But I fear such a recognition will be difficult to get : " a reformer is a person who wants to reform other people, but not himself," Mr. Dooley once cynically remarked ; and I regret to say it contains a large element of truth, for the difficulty which stands in the way of social reform is finally that we are not open to consider any scheme which seriously interferes with the lives to which each one of us seems irrevocably committed. We are town bred, and we don't particularly care for ideas of reform which would turn a great percentage of us into agricultural workers.

I can sympathize with such feelings. I know how difficult it would be for me to abandon town life and to work in the country. And yet intellectual honesty compels me to affirm that, apart from a change in the nature of the activities which make up our lives, there is no solution for our problems. In a really healthy society there would exist a certain ratio between the rural and urban populations. What that ratio should be I am not prepared to say. But that there exists a gross disproportion between the two to-day, few will be found to deny. The present depression in agriculture reacts to aggravate the industrial problem by driving the countryman into the towns to compete with the town worker for a living, and thus, where it does not actually depress the standard rate of wages, prevents the town worker from improving his conditions.

The *New Age* has repeatedly urged the importance of the Trade Unions spending money on organizing the agricultural workers. This is important ; but I would go further than this. I think the Unions would be well advised in financing " back to the land " schemes. They should buy land and use it for the purpose of transferring such of their members as could not find employment in their own trades to agricultural occupations. But the formation of such colonies would need to be preceded by the organization of the agricultural workers in order to diminish the discrepancy in wages.

It will be impossible for me to enter into the details of such a scheme, because with the agricultural problem, as such, I am incompetent to deal. Suffice it to say, however, that I recognize it as the most fundamental of all. Those, however, who are interested in it should study the work of the Irish Agricultural Organization Society. So far as I gather from its literature, the economic problem which confronts the revival of agriculture is parallel to that which confronts the revival of craftsmanship. In each case the middleman stands in the way. The Irish peasant remained poor because the middleman, by standing between him and his market, was in a position to rob him of his earnings, just in the same way as he does the craftsman.

The revival of agriculture would certainly relieve the pressure of competition in our towns. But whether by this means alone a proper ratio between urban and rural areas could be established is very much open to question. I am inclined to think that there are too many of us in this country, and that emigration is necessary to the solution of our problems. In this sense we have a population problem. The Lords of Statistics with their motto : " The more the merrier," refuse to recognize it. But that is because they regard society as an aggregation of individual or atomic units which are as interchangeable as coins, and are utterly destitute of any conception of society as an organism.

To minds so constituted I can quite understand that the population problem has no existence. But it is otherwise with those who, having more insight into the nature of 'men, realize on what terms it is possible for them to co-operate. Like Aristotle, they perceive that the problems of Government increase with an excess of population. The Greeks boldly faced this situation, and when the population of their cities became too big to be manageable, sent out their citizens to establish new colonies. With us emigration is largely left to individual initiative, and the result is not only that we do not emigrate in sufficient numbers, but we emigrate in a wrong spirit. The man who emigrates alone separates from his friends, and rarely settles down in the land of his adoption in the way that Italians and Eastern Europeans do, who always emigrate in groups. He cherishes the hope of making a pile and returning home. It is this spirit that has corrupted colonial life and has brought into existence social problems like our own. There are no cities in the world which suffer more from overcrowding than the Canadian towns. Speculation has raised land values so high that it is only by crowding houses together that building schemes can be made to pay.

The opinion of Aristotle that the problem of government is largely the problem of numbers receives ample support from the writings of Mr. E. L. Godkin. In *Unforeseen Tendencies of Democracy*, Mr. Godkin shows how the decline of the ideal of American Democracy is to be traced ultimately to the increase in the numbers of voters. In the early days of American Democracy, when the voters were few, men of character were personally well known in the community, and such men became public representatives, because of their prominence. But with the rapid increase of emigration the members of society ceased to be well known to each other, and then the trouble began. A capacity for public speaking rather than personal character became the primary qualification for public life, because only good speakers could become sufficiently well known to the electorate. With this change there came a deterioration in the type of public representative, for a capacity for public speaking provides no guarantee for either wisdom or character.

Following this decline of the calibre of the public representative came the growth of the power of the " machine," which could automatically produce majorities in favour of any candidate which it chose to support. With this came political corruption and jobbery. The same kind of thing is happening here. The party system has gradually destroyed the independence of the private member, and can automatically produce majorities ; but we have not sunk so low as America, and it is quite possible that we never shall, for the tradition of public life is much stronger here, and the Englishman is not so single-hearted as is the American in the pursuit of the dollar. But we are travelling in the same direction, and it is necessary for us to pause and think. The evil in each case is the same, namely that the units of organization are too large, so that men can no longer be well known to each other. A healthy public life is impossible when a man ceases to be known to his next-door neighbour, and this phenomenon is the inevitable accompaniment of large cities and large organizations.

XIX

THE REABSORPTION OF THE PROFESSIONS

IT is evident that if the reform of society is to proceed in the direction I have indicated, and small industries and local markets are to take the place of large industries and universal markets, the professions will shrink into comparative insignificance.

In *Civilization: Its Cause and Cure*, Mr. Edward Carpenter contrasts the health, vigour, and immunity from disease of the barbarian with the unhealthiness of civilized man, pointing out, incidentally, that the growth of the number of doctors in our society is not indicative of the increase of health, but of disease. The same principle may be applied to all the professions. Their growth in every case is symptomatic of the growth of disease in one form or another. The growth of the number of lawyers is a sign of the growth of disease in the body politic, while the growth of the number of architects is indicative of the growth of disease in architecture and the building trades. Further, the professions to-day are overcrowded. In every one of them

10

there are many more attempting to earn a living
at them than is warranted by the amount of work
which requires to be done ; from which fact it
appears that the abnormal growth of the professions is itself indicative of a still more serious
disease in the community as a whole.

When we seek for an explanation of this
phenomenon, we find it in the misapplication of
machinery. It is evident that as machine production extends its area, and handicraft is destroyed,
it obliges almost everybody, who is under the
necessity of earning a living, to attempt to get a
footing in the class higher than the one in which
he was born. The immediate effect of machine
production was to increase enormously the number
of commercial travellers, shopkeepers, and middlemen of various kinds. Throughout the nineteenth
century such people who constituted the middle
class became very prosperous, for a large proportion of the increased wealth of the community
found its way into their hands. But a point came
at last when the limit of expansion of this class
was reached, and from that time forward the
increase of the middle class has been accompanied
by an increase in the pressure of competition. As
the rising generation of the middle class could
not go back to handicraft, owing to the spread
of machine production, it has pressed itself forward
into the professions. It is true that other influences
have been at work, such as the desire of the
more prosperous members of the middle class to
secure social prestige by educating their sons for

the professions ; but the economic pressure which' followed the misapplication of machinery has increasingly driven them in this upward direction by forcing upon the rising generation the choice between struggling for a living in the professions or being enslaved as a clerk, or shop assistant, by some large organization which had come about as a result of the increase of competition in the middle class. Needless to say, every member of the class who was in a position to do so chose to fight in the professions.

The fact that the growth of the number of doctors is indicative of the growth of disease is self-evident, and as Mr. Carpenter has dealt with this issue at some length, I will not do more than mention it. But the application of the same principle is not so apparent in the case of lawyers and architects.

Everybody knows that the law to-day does not secure justice. Yet it is only the philosopher who understands that a codified law is incompatible with justice. In England to-day, as in Rome, the idea is that if the law is to be administered impartially it must be administered impersonally. It is supposed that if the judge is personally known to the accused he will be influenced one way or another, and that this will defeat the ends of justice. We have become so accustomed to this way of thinking that we accept it as a dogma. And yet nothing can be further from the truth, for we can only be just to a man when we know his personal character and can enter into the difficulties and circumstances of his life. The member of a class which has command of circumstances, and who enjoys freedom of choice in most of his actions, is rarely able to sympathize with the man who is at the mercy of circumstances. Hence the class prejudice which disgraces the English Bench. The Greeks who worked out the basis of Law—for Greek law underlies the Roman Law—realized the personal nature of justice. Aristotle affirms that justice is only possible in small communities. "The magistrates," he says, " can neither determine causes with justice nor issue their orders with propriety unless they know the character of their fellow-citizens ; so that whenever this happens not to be the case the State must of necessity be badly managed ; for it is not right to determine too hastily and without proper knowledge, as is more or less inevitable if the citizens are too many." Further, he gives us some idea as to the size of such a community. "Ten men," he says, " are too few for a city ; a hundred thousand are too many." And in this connection we should know that by City is implied "State," for the Greek States were City States.

In the village communities, under which agriculture was everywhere organized prior to the growth of Feudalism, such conditions obtained. In them the administration of justice was a personal affair, governed by custom and tradition. According to Kropotkin, "every dispute was brought first before mediators and arbiters, and it mostly ended with them, the arbiters playing a very important part in barbarian society. But if the case was too grave to be settled in this way, it came before the folkmote, which was bound ' to find the sentence ' and pronounce it in a conditional form ; that is, ' such compensation was due if the wrong be proved,' and the wrong had to be proved or disclaimed by six or twelve persons confirming or denying the fact by oath ; ordeal being resorted to in case of contradiction between the two sets of jurors."

Justice to-day has become an aspiration or intellectual concept ; it can only be realized objectively amid primitive conditions of society. The reason for this is that it is only under such conditions that law, morality, and fact are inseparable from each other. The trouble appears to begin when one people is conquered and becomes subject to the domination of another, and the idea of justice gives placê to the idea of how the conquering race can best organize its military superiority for the purposes of orderly government. A people who were actuated primarily by the motive of justice would never seek to become a large State. Unfortunately for the happiness of the world, this motive has rarely been the dominant one. The love of conquest and power has always exercised a fascination for people whose character and circumstances enabled them to gratify it. And so conditions have come into existence under which justice has become a dream rather than a reality, and recourse has been made to law, not with the idea of administering justice, but as a rough-and-ready instrument for the purpose of maintaining order in the external affairs of life. The enforcement of order tends to make law more and more impersonal, and to widen the gulf which separates it from justice.

Such is the reason or basis of the legal profession. The attainment of order rather than justice is the object of its ambition. As such, its existence is symptomatic of the disease of society. In the Greek City States the lawgiver was the philosopher, and it is only on such terms that justice is possible, because alone among men the philosopher sees the reason of things and can relate the idea of justice to human possibilities. The lawyer makes no such pretensions. His love of hair-splitting technicalities, which has made the law a lottery, is itself evidence of a lack of breadth of vision. He follows the line of least resistance, and the line of least resistance in each case is to give legal sanction to what is established, no matter how it has been established. The abandonment of the ideal of justice has been followed by the growth of social confusion, and the growth of confusion involves the extension of legalism. The spread of legalism tends to reduce to impotence every limb of the body politic. It is a vicious circle from which there is no escape apart from a return to first principles.

Any attempt to give application to such first principles in modern society necessarily appears Utopian and impracticable. It would be easy to lay down the principle that every man has a right to be judged by his peers—that such bodies, for instance, as Trade Unions should exercise the rights of jurisdiction over their own members as the Guilds did in the Middle Ages. But the spirit of the age blocks the way. Not until the spirit of competition and mutual suspicion can be replaced by one of co-operation and mutual confidence is such a change to be thought of. In the meantime the evil inherent in the existing legal system should be reduced to a minimum by limiting the fees of the advocate while depriving him of his monopoly of the Bench. Only in the United States of America and this country does the advocate enjoy this monopoly. The promotion of laymen to the Bench would bring a breath of common sense into our fusty legal atmosphere.

XX

THE TRADE DESIGNER

IT will be convenient for us, before considering the profession of the architect, to consider the position of the trade designer. I do not call it a profession, because the trade designer has not the status of the professional man, though the function he is supposed to fulfil is sufficiently important to warrant it.

When we consider that the trade designer is responsible equally with the architect for the design of all those things which combine to make the environment of our lives, it is a strange comment on our social and industrial arrangements that he enjoys no status. He is not recognized as an artist, and yet the abilities needed to perform his function properly are far greater than those required by the average painter, for painting in these days is for the most part an imitative art, whilst design is a creative one, and as such is entitled to take a higher rank. It is, in fact, the very essence of art ; for, strictly speaking, painting only becomes an art when it is used as a medium of expression by men who are conversant with the arts of design.

Yet we gratuitously bestow the title of artist on every imitative dabbler in paint, and not only withhold it from those who pursue a vocation which demands really creative gifts, but are content to condemn them to a lifelong servitude to salesmen and bagmen, who, by dictating to them how things shall be done, have assumed the function of censors of public taste. Nearly all trade designers are in this position. They have become the unwilling slaves of commercial organizations, and the degradation of the products of industrialism bears witness to their servitude. The absence of status of the trade designer has reacted upon himself ; and, generally speaking, he is to-day no better than his position. He has never in his life been given the opportunity of using his gifts in a rational way, and his faculties have become atrophied in consequence.

When Socialists talk about reforming industrialism, I always think of the trade designer, for the possibilities of reform depend finally upon a change in his status, and, if we accept industrialism, I cannot think of any scheme which could possibly alter it for the better. His present subordination is involved in the whole structure of industrialism. Under the old mediæval system of qualitative production the designer, craftsman, and salesman were for the most part one and the same person, and where they were not actually identical they were in such close contact with each other as to work harmoniously together.

The consequence was that the mediæval crafts-

man was independent ; he had some control over
the circumstances of his industry.   But when
quantitative was substituted for qualitative production the designer lost his independence.   Class
divisions came into industry, and so he, separated
from the craftsman, became subject to the control
of the salesman, who in turn was controlled by
the financier.   In this position he will remain
so long as quantitative production obtains, because
with such an ideal it is natural that those who are
primarily concerned with quantitative output will
be in a stronger economic position and take precedence over those whose concern is with the
quality of the wares produced.   So long as the
trade designer remains in this position production
will flounder for the lack of any clear direction ;
for there is, finally, only one man who can direct
the power of industry into its proper channels,
namely the artist, and quantitative production
denies the designer this status.

   This is the dilemma in which modern industry
finds itself.   Literally the tail wags the dog.   A
system of organization which subordinates the
primary functions of designing and making things
to the secondary ones of buying and selling is
clearly on a false basis.   It is fundamentally
unsound, and no sophistry can make it otherwise.
Socialists who imagine that a solution of industrial
problems is possible on a basis of quantitative
production would be required to show how the
four classes of men involved in production to-day
—the financiers, salesmen, designers, and work-

men—could be made to co-operate together. This they can only do by ignoring the psychological problem involved. You cannot have two Cæsars in the same camp, and for the same reason the artist and the financier can never co-operate together except on terms which make them mutually independent of each other. Work together in the same organization they cannot. One of them must rule, and under a system of quantitative production it will be the financier who will do so, as under qualitative production it will be the artist and philosopher. It is the privilege of democracy to decide between them. If it allows its cupidity to be tempted and supports quantitative production, the financier remains to exploit it for its folly. But if on the other hand it supports qualitative production, then power will gradually pass into the hands of the artist and philosopher, and democracy will be rewarded with liberty. For the ideal of the artist is ultimately democratic, though immediately his action is autocratic ; whereas the financier is immediately democratic and ultimately autocratic.

I say, then, that the artist's ideal is democratic. He knows only too well that he cannot save his soul alone. A democratic aim is thrust upon him by the needs of self-existence. He knows that the only terms on which it is finally possible to revive the arts are identical with those which will emancipate the workers from the tyranny of Industrialism. Quantitative production, by destroying craftsmanship, has taken away the ground from under the artist's feet. It has enabled the financier to enslave the designer, and now the evil result is being felt. Without the direction which the artist alone can give, production finds itself to-day at the mercy of every fashion. There is but one remedy for this state of things : to return to the old ways. Economic stability finally rests upon intellectual and æsthetic stability, and these are impossible under a system of production which denies everything fundamental, both in art and in life.

But things are turning in this direction. The tremendous growth of the antique trade is one of the significant developments of the age. It is the answer of the public to the impotence and futility of industrialism. It says in so many words that the present methods of industry are wrong, and that if scientific machinery produces such deplorable results, then, judging by results, the only sensible thing to do is to seek to revive the past. It foreshadows that reaction against the deadlock of modernism which in the sphere of politics finds its immediate expression in the growth of revolutionary feeling, as it will ultimately seek it in a conscious revival of the traditions of the past.

XXI

THE PROFESSION OF ARCHITEC-
TURE

THAT the growth of professionalism is coinci-
dent with the growth of social disease in the case
of the architectural profession as well as in law
and medicine is an opinion that has been held
by the highest authorities. In the year 1892 a
collection of essays by different architects, edited
by Mr. R. Norman Shaw, R.A., and Mr. F. G.
Jackson, R.A., appeared under the provocative
title, *Architecture: A Profession or an Art?* The
object of this book was to affirm the principle
that the only solution of the problems of architecture was to be found in a return to the Mediæval
method of building ; and to prove that the architectural profession should pursue a policy which
in the long run would eventuate in the resumption
by the architect of the position which he occupied
in the Middle Ages as Master of the Works, co-
ordinating the work of a group of craftsmen,
each capable of supplying the details and
ornaments of their own crafts, much in the
same way that the conductor of an orchestra

brings into harmony the efforts of the various musicians.

Any one who is vitally interested in architecture as an art, and is familiar with the economics of the profession, will find it impossible to resist this conclusion, for as it exists to-day the architectural profession has not within itself the elements of permanence. It is manifestly in a state of transition, and must either pursue a policy which will 'aim at the removal of the existing class division between the architect and the building trades, as in the Middle Ages, or the architect must consent to be enslaved by the surveyor. It is probable that at the worst there will be some architects who will be able to escape this fate, owing to exceptional influence. But there is no denying that the general tendency to-day is in this direction, and that just as the architect enslaved the craftsman, so he, in turn, is being enslaved by the surveyor.

Architects, as they existed during Renaissance times, were mainly the exceptional men of the building trades who had become specialized in design because of their superior gifts. They were few in number, and were only employed on the most monumental work ; ordinary buildings were still designed by the master builders. But this is no longer the case. The architectural profession in its present proportions has not come into existence in response to a demand for architecture, but in response to a demand for commercial building. The immediate cause of the rapid expansion was the growth of the contract system in building, which brought into existence a man to enforce the contracts. This man, originally a surveyor or builders' clerk, who knew something about the finance of building, but was without any pretensions to architectural knowledge, began to call himself an architect because he found it commercially advantageous to do so. Important work came to be placed in his hands, but as he was without the knowledge which would have enabled him to make a proper use of his opportunities, he made a terrible mess of things. The problem to-day is how can the minority of real architects leaven this mass of ignorance, which owes its existence to the creation of a class of practitioners who are qualified to fulfil one function, but are entrusted by the public with another for which they are unqualified and which can only be performed successfully by men of quite a different type of mind. This tendency of the profession to draw its recruits from non-architectural sources is the economic problem in architecture.

The profession is flooded with men who are not in the architectural tradition, but come in from the estate agency end of things. In the city and in the suburb, generally speaking, the man who can control the site can control the job. Hence it is that men who are really surveyors and estate agents come to handle great architectural opportunities, while men whose whole training and ability are for architecture often find themselves unable to get near the work at all.

Again, men who have graduated in the building trade never to-day rise to the position of architects at all.

The same tendency is observable in public architects' offices. The head positions are invariably occupied by surveyors masquerading as architects, and if architects are ever to be found there, they are always in inferior positions. The reason for this anomaly is easily understood. The surveyor comes first. He is required by public bodies for road-making, sewering, and other such work. The more utilitarian type of buildings comes to be placed in his hands, and thus he continues until important work comes within his grasp. It is owing to the action of such forces that the surveyor is supplanting the architect to-day.

Little more need be said to demonstrate that the profession of architecture as it exists to-day is on a false basis, and is symptomatic of social disease. There was certainly a case for architects in the past of the type of John Thorpe and Inigo Jones, who were trained as craftsmen, and became specialized in later life as architects, because of their superior gifts of design. But the profession to-day is clearly on a wrong basis, when it would entirely deny opportunities to such men, had they lived to-day and worked in the building trade, whilst offering many opportunities to surveyors and estate agents, and would place men who have been trained as architects, and who do not happen to be men of means and good social position, at the mercy of sheer chance. Obviously there is something wrong, and though within certain limits a remedy for this confusion may be found by the exercise of a wise and discriminating patronage, yet it is apparent that so long as the class division between the architect and the building trades remains, a complete solution is impossible.[1]

The cause of the enslavement of the building trades by the architect was æsthetic, inasmuch as the profession owed its existence to the desire to revive Roman architecture, of which the craftsmen of the building trades were ignorant, and naturally brought into existence a type of man who was conversant with Roman work. The latter-day development which spells the enslavement of the architect by the surveyor and estate agent is economic, and owes its existence finally to the growth of big towns, large organizations, and the contract system. It is the natural and inevitable ending of a false ideal of architecture which has separated the architect from the craftsman. The estate agent has come to stand in the same relation to the architect without social position as the salesman or middleman does to the trade designer. The enslavement of the trade designer came first, because he only designed small things ; the enslavement of the architect is pro-

---

[1] I hope nobody will accuse me of advocating the abolition of the architectural profession. Such would only make matters worse. The transition from the architect to the master builder is necessarily gradual.

11

ceeding to-day. There is no remedy apart from a return to former conditions. Architecture is incompatible with industrialism, and all efforts to graft it on to it must fail in the end.

XXII
THE DESTRUCTIVE CONSUMPTION OF SURPLUS WEALTH

THROUGHOUT this book I have repeatedly urged the importance of social reformers paying more regard to the claims of art, and have drawn attention to the economic implications of its neglect. It is difficult to overestimate the economic confusion which has its origin in the change of fashions consequent upon our national indifference to all questions appertaining to taste. If I have failed to drive this point home I have written in vain, for it is the key to one half of the problems I have discussed. To me, art and economics are as bound together as the soul and the body, which are only to be separated at death. It is no exaggeration to say that the welfare of art is in the end of more importance than morality, for morality is a negative thing, and can only tell us what not to do, whilst art is positive and can tell us what to do. A nation which disregards its claims lacks the means of expression not only in art but in politics as well. It pays for its neglect in a thwarted national and social life and in economic confusion, for it finds itself at the mercy of

forces which it can neither control nor understand. Life which is thwarted returns upon itself
and seeks by underground and illicit means a
way of escape. It is not without significance
that, whilst the greatest achievements of the
Middle Ages were to be found in the temples
for worship, our greatest ones are to be found
in engines of destruction. For the Dreadnought
bears the same relation to the thought and
impulse of this age as the cathedral did to the
Middle Ages—the one is built for the protection
of the body, the other for the protection of the
soul. And it all comes about because as a
nation we are occupied exclusively with material
considerations. We concentrate all our attention
on the means of civilization, to the utter neglect
and disregard of the ends which such means
are to serve. So, instead of public and spiritual
ends, we serve secret and private ones, which
stand in the way of any restoration of a
communal life.

Let no one think that the contrasts I have
drawn are mere idle speculations. They are
only too painfully demonstrable in the terms of
economics. After immediate physical wants are
satisfied, a time comes in the history of every
nation when it finds itself in the possession of
surplus wealth. Its future history and happiness
largely depend upon the use it makes of it. In
the past that surplus was always spent upon
art, and particularly upon architecture. Pericles,
who was perhaps the wisest man who ever held

the reins of power, sought to spend it in this
way. In answer to some who complained that
Athens was over-adorned, like a woman wearing
too many jewels, he replied that surplus wealth
was best spent in such works as would bring
eternal glory to the city, and at the same time
employ her artificers. In the Middle Ages
surplus wealth was spent upon building
cathedrals, and the custom of spending it
on the arts obtained in history until modern
times. Following the triumph of Protestantism
and the plundering of the Church lands, there
came a relaxation of the mediæval laws against
usury in order to accommodate morals to the
practice of the rich, and along with it came
an increased private and a decreased public
expenditure upon architecture. Still the surplus
continued to be spent mainly in this way, and
it was not until the introduction of machinery
that a change gradually took place. From that
time forward surplus wealth came to be spent
less and less upon building and more and more
upon new productive enterprises ; or, in other
words, it ceased to be consumed, but was re-
invested for the purposes of a further increase,
until in our day the proper expenditure of
surplus wealth has been entirely lost sight of.
When people build nowadays they no longer
regard it as a means of consuming a surplus,
but as a speculation by which they hope to
increase their riches, and this applies not only
to building, but to pictures, which are bought

to-day as investments. This changed attitude is really the financial difficulty connected with the housing problem, for it is only in modern times that houses were ever expected to pay.

But the evil does not end here. As few people nowadays have any disposition to spend their surplus in the right way, and as almost everybody seeks to use it as a means of further increase, the balance which in former times existed between demand and supply has been utterly destroyed, and the pressure of competition has increased. Indirectly this results in an increase of personal expenditure, for such increase among the well-to-do is necessitated by the need of the individual holding his own in the competitive social world, which in turn is necessitated by the need of securing opportunities for the making of more wealth, and in the professional classes of a living. Hence the general meanness of people in regard to expenditure upon things of permanent value, and hence again our ever-increasing national expenditure upon armaments, which is due to the pressure of competition among nations. It is a vicious circle from which there is no escape so long as people misuse their surplus wealth. They decline to spend it on the arts because it is unremunerative, and in the end they are compelled to spend it on armaments, which are not only unremunerative but a peril to their own existence. To such a pass have we been brought by our faith in a political economy which teaches

that greed and usury are the pillars of the State !
It is the judgment of God, and who can deny
its justice?

Our misuse of surplus wealth accounts for
our excessive use of machinery. Had we never
lost sight of the ends which production sub-
serves we should have had need of very little
machinery. If we had continued to look upon
architecture and craftsmanship as a means of
consuming surplus wealth we should have realized
the utter absurdity of allowing machinery to
trespass on its domains from the economic as
well as from the æsthetic point of view. As it
is, our surplus wealth is spent less and less
upon the production of those things which in
the past were regarded as among the ends of
civilization, and more and more upon the
machinery of production. Nay, we have gone
farther ; the more recent development is
machinery for the purpose of making machinery.
This I can only call the destructive consumption
of surplus wealth. We have lost the art of consuming it and have developed the art of destroying it ; for that, indeed, is the task upon which
we are engaged to-day. Hence it is, when men
like Mr. H. G. Wells and Sir Leo Chiozza
Money imagine that the way to remedy the evils
of poverty is to increase the use of machinery,
they exhibit themselves as the mere slaves of
circumstance, as is natural with men who concentrate all their attention on the means of
civilization and disregard the ends.

Fortunately for me, I am able to point to two modern economists who have held the same idea, though they have expressed themselves differently.   Mr. J. A. Hobson, in his analysis of the unemployed problem, came to the conclusion that the solution was to be found in raising the standard of production, which amounts to much the same thing ; whilst Mr. J. M. Robertson held a similar idea, as readers of his *Fallacy of Saving* will know.   Unfortunately, neither of them was familiar with the economics of the arts, and so failed to reduce their conclusions to concrete terms.   But their testimony is valuable as showing that, from whatever point of view the modern problem is approached, careful analysis brings us to the same conclusion.

XXIII

ON PROPERTY

THERE are two ways of analysing the structure of society. We may begin with the nature of man and reason to his environment, or we may reverse the process. The former is the method of the Guildsman, the latter of the Collectivist. But just as the Collectivist, reasoning from environment, must come, in the end, to definite conclusions about the nature of man, so the Guildsman will finally have something to say about property, and, as may be expected, he will come to different conclusions.

It goes without saying that the present-day distribution of property is absolutely indefensible ; but that admission does not mean that we must accept the Collectivist solution of the problem. We may agree that, in an ideal state of society, goods would be held in common, and that in the distant future such an ideal may be realized, and yet recognize that it is altogether incompatible with a highly complex state of society. Any attempt to give practical application to such a principle would, at the present time, lead to greater evils than those from which we now suffer ; for in practical affairs we must reckon with men as they are, and with the problem as it exists, both in regard to the evils to be eradicated and the forces at our disposal for the purpose of reform. We must recognize that the spirit of avarice pervades our society ; that those in possession of property are powerful ; and that as most of those who desire a different state of affairs live under constant economic pressure it is exceedingly difficult for them, with the best intentions, to act in an entirely disinterested way. These are the factors in the present situation, and they are sufficient to make any transition to Collectivism impracticable, even if it were desirable, which in this connection I am persuaded it is not.

I insist upon a frank recognition of these facts because it is only on such terms that it will be possible for us to handle the present situation with any measure of success. Though we may recognize that communism is not immediately practicable, let us not lose sight of the fact that it is our goal ; for we may test the value of any idea based upon the necessity of compromise by reference to it. If it strengthens personal and human ties, then it is making for communism, for communism is only possible when men and women are bound together in such ways. But if it ignore this necessity, and seek to substitute for such ties the impersonal activity of the State, then it is a certainty that such ideas will, in their ultimate workings, prove to be anti-communal. This is my objection to the nationalization of property. It involves bureaucracy, and as bureaucracy is the impersonal instrument of the State, it stands condemned as an anti-communal form of organization.

Recognizing then on the one hand that the nationalization of property is not only impracticable but undesirable, and on the other that we have become too individualistic in temperament to render organization on a communist basis practicable for the time being, common sense suggests the desirability of reviving the Mediæval attitude towards property, which steers a safe middle course between the impracticable and the undesirable. The Mediæval economists, who appear to have debated the question of property very thoroughly, finally threw over Plato's idea of *common property and private use* in favour of Aristotle's idea of *private property and common use*, which they considered more suitable to this workaday world. They thought that common property was suitable for a religious community each member of which accepted a discipline, but not for those who were unprepared to do so. St. Thomas Aquinas held that private property was necessary for three reasons. " Firstly, because every one is more solicitous about procuring what belongs to himself alone than that which is common to all or many, since each, shunning labour, leaves to another what is the common burden of all, as happens with a multitude of servants. Secondly, because human affairs are conducted in a more orderly fashion if each has his own duty of procuring a certain thing, while there would be confusion if each should procure things haphazard. Thirdly, because in this way the peace of men is better preserved, for each is content with his own. Whence we see that strife more frequently arises among those that hold a thing in common and undividedly. The other office which is a man's concerning exterior things is the use of them ; and with regard to this a man ought not to hold exterior things as his own, but common to all, that he may portion them out to others readily in time of need."

Mediæval economists accepted private property as a convenient arrangement for managing human affairs. But they did not consider possession as absolute. A man held property in trust for the commonweal.[1] To succour the needy was enjoined upon them, and to withhold alms under certain circumstances was to commit mortal sin. St. Thomas Aquinas, along with others, held that in case of urgent necessity a man might take the property of another either openly or secretly, and it was not to be considered as theft. St. Ambrose says, " More than is sufficient for one's need is wrongfully held " : while St. Antonino insisted that should the need arise the State might take over the common ownership of all the forms of wealth,

[1] Since these words were written this principle has been defined as the principle of *function* by Mr. de Maeztu in *Authority, Liberty, and Function in the Light of the War.*

but he regards such a State as violent and impracticable, though not contrary to justice.

The opinions of the Mediævalists in this connection are interesting. If St. Antonino considered that State ownership was impracticable, and mediæval thinkers were all agreed that average human nature was not then sufficiently noble to render possible the common ownership of wealth, are we justified in considering it more practicable to-day, when the spirit of avarice reigns supreme, and when experience has proved it impossible to provide by checks and counter-checks against the abuses of dishonest men? Obviously, before common ownership is practicable a change would need to come over the spirit of society, and if such a change came about the need would no longer be felt. Looked at from this point of view, the proposal to nationalize property seems to partake more of the nature of a protest against the monstrous injustice of present-day economic arrangements than a practical administrative proposition. The experience of history appears to prove that the common ownership of land is possible within the limits of a village community ; and I think it would be possible for small local Guilds to own property in the form of houses, etc., and no harm would come. But if the Guilds were large, I feel sure common ownership would destroy the liberty of the individual. Common property ceases to be desirable at that point when a community becomes too large for the individuals who compose it to be personally well known to each other. Moreover, it is not desirable to forbid private property for another reason. Society is largely dependent for its vitality upon the public-spirited action of individuals who are in a position of comparative independence. Men may circulate new ideas though they have no property, but their reduction to practice depends ultimately upon the action of men who are economically independent. It is necessary to have a sure footing in the material world if a man is to affect material results. To what extent this will be necessary in the future it is impossible to say ; but there is no denying that it holds good to-day, and will do so for a considerable time to come.

XXIV

THE LEISURE AND WORK STATES

THE final test as to whether a man is a Collectivist or a Guildsman is to be found in his
partiality for the Leisure or the Work State.
If he favours the Leisure State, then he will be
found to be at heart a Collectivist, while if he
is a Guildsman he will have nothing to do
with it.

It is easy, of course, to understand why the
Leisure State should have the more popular
appeal of the two conceptions. It appeals to
the immediate needs of the majority. More
leisure connotes less toil, and for the majority
who are slave-driven it appears to offer them
immediate relief from the oppression they suffer.
Nevertheless, I am persuaded that it is an utterly
impossible dream so far as the majority are
concerned, and that their salvation is not to
be found in a policy which, accepting present
conditions of labour, aims at reducing working
hours to a minimum—the ideal of the advocates
of the Leisure State—but rather in the humaniza-
tion of labour which we associate with the Work
State.

I have associated the idea of the Leisure State with Collectivist ways of thinking because it seems to me to involve another state—the Servile State. To me the Leisure State and the Servile State are complementary—the one involves the other. I cannot conceive of a state of society in which everybody lived a life of idleness and pleasure, because the pursuit of pleasure inevitably leads to selfishness. "It is fitting," says St. Thomas Aquinas, "that there should be some pleasure in human intercourse, as it were a condiment, so that the soul of man may be refreshed." But this is a fundamentally different thing from the organization of society on a basis of pleasure, for pleasure, if it is to be really enjoyed, must not be pursued as an end in itself, but must come as a by-product, as it were, of virtuous activity. The pursuit of pleasure defeats its own purpose, for in the long run it destroys the possibility of further pleasure. It leads to boredom and finally to selfishness because, softened by delights, men become lazy. The very thought of work becomes irksome to them, and in that frame of mind they have neither the will nor the inclination to do their share of the work of the community. They would seek to evade their responsibilities, and to transfer on to the shoulders of others burdens which are disagreeable to them. Thus the Leisure State would only intensify present social evils, by giving permanence to a state of things in which the work of the community is not distributed equally among its members, but is done by those whose economic necessity leaves them no option in the matter—or, in other words, it leads to the Servile State. Nay, is not precisely the pursuit of pleasure to-day the instrument which is bringing into existence the Servile State? The desire for wealth is, so far as the majority are concerned, the desire for pleasure and luxury. For a century or more the reward held out to labour has been its release from the necessity of work, and nowadays, when this spirit has come to pervade the whole community, labour is treated with a measure of callousness and brutality such as civilization never witnessed before.

The civilization of ancient Greece, which approximated in some degree to the Leisure State, was based upon slavery. The Greeks were a logically minded people. Their ideal, in so far as it was formulated, was that of the perfect soul in the perfect body. But realizing that the perfection of the body was incompatible with manual labour, they preferred to compromise with the demands of the soul, and so they frankly accepted the institution of slavery, while they sought to justify this compromise by asserting that some men were slaves by nature. With them excellence was for the few, not for the many. The modern man is incapable of such cold-blooded logic. He always thinks he can have things both ways. He thinks it is possible for every one to enjoy a life of leisure and have

servile conditions of labour abolished at the same
time, and the reason he can entertain this idea
is because he' thinks the introduction of machinery,
has, by increasing the possibilities of quantitative
output, removed the only limitation which made
the Greek ideal incompatible with democracy.

But in this he is mistaken.   Machinery can
never alter the laws of morality.   It is all very
well to argue in the abstract that with the proper
application of machinery labour might be reduced
to three or two hours a day.   But in the concrete
things work out differently.   However much in
theory we may divorce economics from morals,
in practice they are never so divorced.   The
two go hand in hand, and it is only by frankly,
recognizing this fact that it is possible to calcu-
late with any degree of precision in human
affairs.   The fact that servile labour tends to
produce servile men—that it debases the currency of labour—cannot be altered.   Reasonable
pleasure has its basis in reasonable work, and
if men are turned into machines, or are engaged
in mechanical occupations which bring them no
pleasure, then their life is corrupted at its roots.
It matters little if that work be reduced to four
or even two hours a day, the corruption will
be there all the same, and it will corrupt the
leisure which accompanies it.   For at the centre
of life there will be a vacuum which requires
to be filled, and the demon of selfishness will
enter in, for men who are not happy in their
work will be incapable of resistance.   Their

whole thought will be fixed on the pleasures outside, and to secure that pleasure they will be found ready to sacrifice the lives of those who are not so fortunately placed.

I said that the Greek States were Leisure States. This statement needs qualification. We must not forget that the Greek States were also military States. The practice of military exercises occupied much of their leisure, while the ever-constant fear of foreign invasion imposed on them a discipline. It was this which held them together. No sooner was this fear of invasion dispelled and the Leisure State definitely, inaugurated than the Greek States immediately, fell to pieces. The final defeat of the Persian army at Platæa marks the beginning of the decline of Greek civilization. Prior to that battle the Greeks had lived in fear of a Persian invasion, and their whole life had been ordered to meet the needs of warfare. But when at last the Persians had been defeated the whole atmosphere changed. The growth of foreign trade and the luxuries which followed it everywhere undermined their military virtues. Relieved from the necessity of manual labour and without a religion which, by appealing to their hearts and consciences, might exalt the ideal of self-restraint, there was no power to check them once they, were fairly embarked on the pursuit of pleasure. Indeed, the history of Greece, as of Rome, demonstrates clearly that the Pagan ideal of self-sufficiency and self-assertiveness on a basis of

sensuous enjoyment is not an ideal by which
society can live. It could not save its followers
from moral enervation, dissatisfaction with life,
and corruption. Such was the end of the Leisure
State in the past, and such, I am persuaded,
will be the fate of the Leisure State at which
so-called social reformers are aiming. It will
fall to pieces from lack of any stability of
character, for every society needs a discipline
if it is to be stable. If it is not imposed from
within, it will need to be imposed from without.
But the Modernist hates the very thought of
discipline, as, indeed, every other reality. He
will have his deserts.

XXV

CONCLUSION

IN bringing this analysis to a close, my immediate purpose will have been served if I succeed in impressing upon Socialists the fact that the solution of the social problem is not quite so simple a matter as probably the majority have been accustomed to suppose—that the confusion which has followed attempts to give practical application to their principles is for the most part due to the fact that they do not finally touch reality. For though it may be admitted that the present distribution of wealth, involving extremes of riches and poverty, is an evil of the first magnitude, such maldistribution is yet only the outward and visible sign of an inward and spiritual disease. Any political activity which would treat the social problem as a purely materialist issue is doomed from its first inception.

But will come the objection : Granted that the social problem is as complex as I have shown it to be, it is, nevertheless, necessary for the practical purposes of reform to make a selection from the many problems which our society presents, and to concentrate upon them, if anything is to be accomplished. To this I answer that there is no objection to such a selection being made, providing that attempts are not made to effect by political effort changes which can only follow success in other spheres of activity, and that the importance of other forms of activity be not underrated, especially such as aim at the stimulation of thought. The crystallization of the thought and practical activities of the movement around purely material issues is to be traced back to the struggle between William Morris and Mr. Sidney Webb and their supporters in the 'eighties, which decided the subsequent history of the movement. The issue which brought that struggle to a head was whether or no the movement should organize itself for political action. Morris and his supporters opposed this new development, insisting that, for some time to come, not politics but education should be the order of the day. But they were defeated, and from that day forward it became increasingly the policy of the movement to suppress within itself all forms of intellectual activity which were subversive to the political propaganda. Considering the many crazy notions which in those days masqueraded under the cloak of Socialism, there may perhaps have been some justification for the political propagandists, and no harm might have come of the suppression had it been merely an expedient for effecting certain temporary purposes. But once the movement was fairly embarked on political activity, it seemed to have no further use for ideas as such, with the result that it became first intellectually sterile and then politically impotent. Embarking on political activity before a firm foundation of clear thinking had been laid, compromise became inevitable. The demand for great and fundamental changes receded more and more into the background, while the advocacy of palliatives became increasingly the order of the day. To correct this tendency there is but one thing to be done. The movement must for the present abandon its political aspirations, and seek to fortify itself by a return to fundamentals, since, until a basis of clear thinking has been well and securely laid, it is impossible with safety to advocate practical measures at all, because it is certain they will be misapplied. Nay, until such a foundation is laid, practical measures remain impracticable, because their significance will not be understood by the people. Quack remedies will be more acceptable to them.

Among the ideas the suppression of which has led to the present intellectual sterility of the movement is the doctrine of catastrophism. It is easy to understand why the Fabian Society sought to discredit it. If the Socialist movement was to enter the political arena, it could only do so on the assumption that existing society could be reformed. Catastrophism denied such a possibility. It affirmed that the disease of our society had proceeded so far that a cure apart from the total destruction of the existing social order was out of the question. Accordingly, it happened that the Fabian Society substituted evolution for revolution as the watchword of reform. They thought it a fine thing to do, but experience has proved the contrary. The denial of catastrophism not only so emasculated Socialist doctrine as to rob it of all virility, but strangled all new thought within the movement. This was just what might have been expected. Deny the possibility of a catastrophic ending of modern tendency, and the revolutionary spirit goes with it. The reformer must take existing society in its main essentials for granted. All that is left for him to do is to devise schemes for the amelioration of social conditions ; he cannot attack the disease at its source because he is no longer permitted to question things fundamental to the existing social order.

Sufficient has perhaps been said to drive home the fact that if the movement is to recover its old time virility, it must, before all things, re-affirm the catastrophic doctrine. But it must reaffirm it with a difference, for the Marxian theory was only partly true. As I explained in the article on *National Guilds and the General Strike,* Marx was right in predicting the catastrophic ending of the industrial system, but he was wrong in assuming that out of the unemployed a force for revolution could be created.[1] Marx's error of judgment had a most unfortunate influence upon the policy of his followers, for it led them

[1] See footnote to page 56.

to oppose all measures for the temporary allevia-
tion of existing distress, on the assumption that
palliatives would tend to delay the coming of
revolution. Such a policy was inhuman, and it
is not surprising that the majority of Socialists
shrank from giving unqualified support to a
doctrine so incompatible with their better feelings. But with us it will be different. For being
of the opinion that when the revolution does come
it will follow an impact from without, in reviving the doctrine of catastrophism we shall
not feel ourselves committed to such a policy,
for palliatives would be unable to prevent its
coming.

Such, then, is the parting of the ways. The
choice which we have to make is whether we
accept existing society in its main essentials in
the belief that the evils which it has brought
into existence may be abolished ; or whether,
convinced that the evils are organic with the very
structure of society, we seek to replace existing
society by a society based upon the civilization
of the past. If the latter be our choice, we
shall become stronger. We shall gain in clarity
of vision and certainty of aim. But if such be
not the case, and we still keep on saying " We
cannot go back," then all I can say is that we
must go forward to increasing misery, to increasing confusion, to increasing despair ; and
finally to that recrudescence of barbarism which
science is to-day restoring under the mask of civilization. For no pretence that things are other-

wise, no compromise with things as they are, can save us from that great and universal catastrophe in which the civilization of industrialism will find its inevitable ending.

Printed in Great Britain by
UNWIN BROTHERS, LIMITED, THE GRESHAM PRESS, WOKING AND LONDON

Towards Industrial Freedom

By EDWARD CARPENTER

Crown 8vo.   *Paper, 2s. 6d. net.*   *Cloth, 3s. 6d. net.*

This new work by Mr. Edward Carpenter, consisting of a series of papers on the subject of the new organizations and new principles which will, it is hoped, be established in the world of Industry after the war, will be eagerly welcomed by all thoughtful people.

The Present Position and Power of the Press

By HILAIRE BELLOC

Crown 8vo.   *2s. 6d. net.*   *Postage 5d.*

The purpose of this essay is to discuss the evils of the great modern Capitalist Press, its function in vitiating and misinforming opinion, and in putting power into ignoble hands; its correction by the formation of small independent organs, and their probably increasing effect.

Economic Conditions

1815 and 1914

Crown 8vo.   By H. R. HODGES, B.Sc. (Econ.)   *2s. 6d. net.*

A book of facts concerning a century's progress in the material welfare of the people of England, comparing their economic position and power, occupations and remuneration at the end of one great European war and the outbreak of a greater.

The book, with its interesting tables and diagrams, gives a clear picture of the improvement, and it will also refresh the memories of the conditions and outlook of the people in the last days of peace.

The True Cause of the Commercial Difficulties of Gt. Britain

By CECIL BALFOUR PHIPSON

Edited by Mark B. F. Major and Edward W. Edsall

Crown 8vo.   *2s. 6d. net.*   *Postage 3d.*

This work discloses an unconsidered (but surprisingly obvious) factor in the fiscal controversy, showing that since the internationalization of gold the principles of Free Trade have ceased to operate, and that for their restoration Great Britain must regain the use of a purely national money standard, such as she used prior to 1874, when her commercial prosperity was phenomenal.

Home Truths about the War

By the Rev. HUGH B. CHAPMAN, Chaplain of the Savoy

Crown 8vo.   *2s. 6d. net.*   *Postage 4d.*

An effort to arrive at the psychology of the war so far as it affects ordinary people, and to assert with humour, but without bitterness, truths to which many are longing to give expression. The object of the writer is to insist on the fact that at this moment the combination of patriotism and piety is the one lesson of the war.

The Menace of Peace

By GEORGE D. HERRON. Crown 8vo. 2s. 6d. net. Postage 4d.

The purpose of "The Menace of Peace" is to show that the war is but the outward expression of a human conflict that is spiritual, and the issue of which will decide destiny for long centuries to come. The world is at the cross-roads of history, and is there summoned to decide between the democratic principle represented, however unconsciously, by the Allies, and the autocratic principle, consciously represented by the Central Powers. The war, in its last analysis, is between elemental earth-forces incarnated in Germany and the Christ principle which has slowly and even doubtfully gained recognition in the democratic countries. For the war to close, and the world not know what it has been fighting about, would be the supreme catastrophe of history. A compromise between the contending belligerents would be a betrayal of the peoples of every nation, and would issue in universal mental and moral confusion, and the millions who have died would have died in vain. The supreme opportunity of man would have proven itself greater than man.

The Future of Constantinople

By LEONARD S. WOOLF

Crown 8vo.   *2s. 6d. net.*   *Postage 4d.*

This work deals with one of the most vital problems of British foreign policy, the settlement of the Ottoman Empire after the war. It proposes and discusses a settlement of Constantinople based upon the political, economic, and strategic interests not of one nation, but of all nations. The possibility of its administration by an international organ, modelled on the European Commission of the Danube, is examined in detail, and the history and achievements of the Danube Commission are for the first time in this book made fully available for English readers.

National Defence   A Study in Militarism

By J. RAMSAY MACDONALD, M.P.

Crown 8vo.   THIRD IMPRESSION.   *2s. 6d. net.*   *Postage 4d.*

This book discusses in an original and forceful way the problem of National Defence and International Peace. Mr. Macdonald is not content to restate the familiar arguments of pacifists drawn from the sentiments outraged by war, but boldly faces the military problems of national defence as a student of military writers.

Bohemia's
Case for Independence
By EDWARD BENEŠ, D.Litt.
Lecturer at Prague University, etc, etc.
With an Introduction by HENRY WICKHAM STEED
Foreign Editor of *The Times.*

Crown 8vo.   *2s. 6d. net.*

A clever exposition of the Czecho-Slovak claim for independence from the historical, economic, and political point of view. It reveals Austrian terrorism in Bohemia during the war and proves that the dismemberment of the Dual Monarchy is the only solution if a permanent peace in Europe is to be established.

The United States and the
War   By GILBERT VIVIAN SELDES

Crown 8vo.   *2s. 6d. net.*   *Postage 4d.*

" The United States and the War " is an explanation of what the United States has done and has not done since August 1914. The explanation is found, not in the political efforts of individuals, but in the traditions and social ideals of the American people themselves. On the same basis the book discusses the possible relations of the United States with the liberal nations of Europe. The author is an American journalist now living in England.

The American League to
Enforce Peace
By C. R. ASHBEE
With an Introduction by G. LOWES DICKINSON

Crown 8vo.   *2s. 6d. net.*   *Postage 5d.*

The American League to Enforce Peace, a study of whose objects by Mr. C. R. Ashbee we publish, may turn out to be one of the great land marks of the war. It will sever the United States from their traditional policy, and bring them into a new comity of nations. The American challenge is to every democracy in Europe and it was significant that the League was inaugurated in May 1915 in Independence Hall, the historic home of the signing of the Declaration of Independence. Mr. Ashbee, who, with one exception, was the only Englishman present at the League's inauguration, goes into the question of its policy and the *force* that underlies it (it is no peace campaign).

A Bulwark against Germany

The Fight of the Slovenes, the Western Branch of the Jugoslavs, for National Existence

By BOGUMIL VOSNJAK

Late Lecturer of the University of Zagreb (Croatia).

TRANSLATED BY FANNY S. COPELAND

Crown 8vo.   *4s. 6d. net. Postage 5d.*

After the dismemberment of the Habsburg Empire the union of the Jagoslav nation—the Serbs, Croats, and Slovenes—in one State will be one of the most important features of future Europe. From the beginning of the Middle Ages down to the present great war the western-most branch of this nation, the Slovenes, have waged a brave struggle against German imperialism. The "Bulwark" explains the historical, political, social, and economical evolution of the Slovenes, who will be a strong factor in the building up of the great Serbia or Jugoslavia of to-morrow.

A Dying Empire

By BOGUMIL VOSNJAK

WITH A PREFACE BY T. P. O'CONNOR, M.P.

Crown 8vo.   *4s. 6d. net. Postage 5d.*

In this account of the Dying Empire of Austria the author has tried to describe the sociological factors in the breakdown of the Hapsburg Empire, and to show that in the fabric of a "Central Europe" is closely woven the idea of a predominating Pan-Germanism. Either Germany must stretch from Hamburg to Trieste and Salonika, or Austria-Hungary must be dismembered. There is no alternative.

Poland Past and Present

Crown 8vo.   By J. H. HARLEY   *4s. 6d. net. Postage 5d.*

Some new and vital details of the recent history of this unfortunate country are conveyed to British readers in Mr. J. H. Harley's vividly interesting volume. It is preceded by a preface from the pen of Mr. Ladislas Mickiewicz—the son of the great Polish poet—which states the attitude of the Polish people to Germany, and reveals how deeply their sympathies are enlisted in the cause of the Allies. A notable feature of the book is a record of the attempts made by the Germans in Poland during the last few months to seduce Poland from her confidence in the justice of the Western Powers.

Democracy After the War

By J. A. HOBSON

Crown 8vo. 4*s.* 6*d. net.*

It is the writer's object to indicate the nature of the struggle which will confront the public of this country for the achievement of political and industrial democracy when the war is over. The economic roots of Militarism and of the confederacy of reactionary influences which are found supporting it—Imperialism, Protectionism, Conservatism, Bureaucracy, Capitalism—are subjected to a critical analysis. The safeguarding and furtherance of the interests of Improperty and Profiteering are exhibited as the directing and moulding influences of domestic and foreign policy, and their exploitation of other more disinterested motives is traced in the conduct of Parties, Church, Press, and various educational and other social institutions. The latter portion of the book discusses the policy by which these hostile forces may be overcome and Democracy may be achieved, and contains a vigorous plea for a new free policy of popular education.

The Framework of a Lasting Peace

Demy 8vo. EDITED BY LEONARD S. WOOLF 4*s.* 6*d.*

This work contains a collection of all the more important schemes which have been put forward in America, Britain, and on the Continent for a League of Nations which shall have as its object the reconstruction of international society and the prevention of war. Mr. Woolf, in an Introduction, subjects the different proposals to a critical examination, and shows that upon the most important points they are in substantial agreement, and thus indicate the lines of international agreement which practical statesmanship ought to follow after the war.

Practical Pacifism and its Adversaries : "Is it Peace, Jehu ?"

By Dr. SEVERIN NORDENTOFT
WITH AN INTRODUCTION BY G. K. CHESTERTON

Crown 8vo. 4*s.* 6*d. net. Postage* 5*d.*

In addition to making definite suggestions as to the lines on which the Peace Movement should go to work after the war—suggestions which are both obvious and practical—the book contains a reprint of a pamphlet written by an upper-class native of Schleswig, with footnote criticisms by a Prussian scholar of unbiassed views, which renders very sensational and personal testimony to the terrible discontent and bitter rage which a conquered nation feels in its humiliating position of subjection—thus proving beyond all doubt that the chief obstacle that the Peace Movement has to face is this unnatural denial to the conquered people of the Rights of Peace.

The Choice Before Us

By G. LOWES DICKINSON

Demy 8vo.   *6s. net. Postage 6d.*

This book describes briefly the prospect before the world, if the armed international anarchy is to continue, and to be extended and exasperated, after the war. It analyses and discusses the presuppositions which underlie Militarism. And having argued both that international war as it will be conducted in the future implies the ruin of civilization, and that it is not "inevitable," sketches the kind of reorganization that is both possible and essential if war is not to destroy mankind.

Principles of Social Reconstruction   3RD IMPRESSION

By BERTRAND RUSSELL, F.R.S.

Demy 8vo, 6s. net   Postage 6d.

"Mr. Russell has written a big and living book."—*The Nation.*

Professionalism & Originality

With Some Suggestions for National Reconstruction

By F. H. HAYWARD, D.LITT., B.SC.

Inspector of Schools, Author of "Educational Administration and Criticism,"

Demy 8vo.   *6s. net. Postage 5d.*

This work is an attempt to ascertain and tabulate the signs or stigmata of the conventional (" professional ") man and the contrasted stigmata of the creative ("original") man. Various suggestions bearing on professional and national efficiency are appended. In view of the privileged and almost irresponsible positions occupied by the legal, medical, and other professions, and of the obscurity in which questions of professional superintendence and criticism are involved, the work is likely to prove of considerable importance. Ample quotations are made from contemporary events and literature.

LONDON: GEORGE ALLEN & UNWIN LIMITED

www.ingramcontent.com/pod-product-compliance
Lightning Source LLC
Chambersburg PA
CBHW021209290526

45796CB00006B/32